CONTEMPORARY LOGISTICS IN CHINA

An Introduction

Editors

Binglian Liu
Nankai University, China

Shao-ju Lee
Nankai University, China
Dong Hwa University, Taiwan

Zhilun Jiao
Nankai University, China

Ling Wang
Nankai University, China

World Scientific

NEW JERSEY · LONDON · SINGAPORE · BEIJING · SHANGHAI · HONG KONG · TAIPEI · CHENNAI

Published by

World Scientific Publishing Co. Pte. Ltd.

5 Toh Tuck Link, Singapore 596224

USA office: 27 Warren Street, Suite 401-402, Hackensack, NJ 07601

UK office: 57 Shelton Street, Covent Garden, London WC2H 9HE

British Library Cataloguing-in-Publication Data
A catalogue record for this book is available from the British Library.

CONTEMPORARY LOGISTICS IN CHINA
An Introduction

ISBN-13 978-981-4365-88-8
ISBN-10 981-4365-88-2

Typeset by Stallion Press
Email: enquiries@stallionpress.com

Printed in Singapore.

Contents

Preface

With the rapid development of China's economy in the past decade, there arises a great demand for a comprehensive report concerning the state of development of logistics in China. Yet an English publication on the subject has been wanting. Meeting this need now is the English version of the *China Logistics Development Report*, renamed *Contemporary Logistics in China: An Introduction*, which will serve as an indispensable document for researchers, academicians and all interested in grasping a deeper understanding of logistics in China.

The *China Logistics Development Report* (called the *Blue Book* for short in China) is authored and compiled by the Logistics Research Center at Nankai University, with the express approval and authorization of the Central Government of China. Since the publication of the first report in 2002, eight subsequent reports have been published on an annual basis, covering the progress, status and significant events in logistics for the decade. Among comparable reports in this field, the *Blue Book* is regarded as the most systematic, objective and authoritative publication. *Contemporary Logistics in China: An Introduction* is the first English edition of the *Blue Book*, written specifically for global readers. This timely publication aims to reflect the state of modern logistics in China since the outbreak of the global financial crisis in 2009.

The publication comprises seven chapters. The first three chapters contain syntheses of the features of China's economic development, the development of the logistics market in China and China's logistics infrastructure, thus providing readers with a big picture of the development of logistics in China. In addition, the first three chapters include a comprehensive analysis of the state of China's economy, shedding light on the broader environment in which the development of the logistics industry in China has taken place. The chapters also include a comprehensive assessment of the development of the industry as well as relevant statistics and perspectives regarding the development of China's infrastructure as it relates to logistics.

Given the pronounced regional differences in China's vast geography, an exploratory study of its logistics by major regions would afford the readers a more focused understanding of the characteristics of regional logistics. Hence, the fourth chapter features a comparative analysis of the development of logistics among the Eastern, Central and Western regions, as well as that in the key coastal areas of the Yangtze River Delta, the Pearl River Delta and the Pan-Bohai Area.

Professions related to the logistics industry are also considered an important aspect of China's logistics. The fifth chapter considers the development of retail chains, automotive logistics, as well as petroleum logistics, depicting the development of logistics operations and management of these economic sectors/industries, their existing problems and ongoing trends.

The book also explores some hot topics in logistics that involve major events with important social and economic ramifications. Topics covered in Chapter 6 include emergency logistics (giving special attention to the recent Wenchuan and Yushu earthquakes), events logistics (focusing on the 2008 Olympics) and foreign trade logistics. The goal is to enable the reader to obtain a deeper, fuller understanding of the events that shaped the logistics industry in China in 2009. Chapter 7 concludes with a summary of the covered subjects and a perspective for the future of logistics in China.

This book presents the results of a cohesive and integrative study conducted by a team of seasoned researchers, each knowledgeable in their respective subjects. The Logistics Research Center at Nankai University is committed to continue publishing the most relevant and well-founded information on logistics development in China. This publication is intended to provide useful and in-depth information to scholars and researchers interested in the development of logistics in China, but it could also serve as a handy reference for global enterprises in formulating logistics-related business strategies. Furthermore, the pertinent statistics, legal policies and critical regulations contained herein would expectedly be useful to universities, research institutions, media agencies and governmental departments.

List of Chapter Editors

Chapter 1   Ling Wang, Nankai University

Chapter 2   Xiaomei Jiang, Tianjin Normal University

Chapter 3   Zhilun Jiao, Nankai University

Chapter 4

4.1   Lanbing Li, Nankai University

4.2   Lanbing Li, Nankai University

4.3   Minglei Ding, Nankai University

4.4   Yong Liu, Nankai University

4.5   Minglei Ding, Nankai University

Chapter 5

5.1   Weilin Liu, Tianjin University

5.2   Weihua Liu, Tianjin University

5.3   Maolin Wang, Tianjin Foreign Studies University

Chapter 6

6.1   Xiang Li, Nankai University
6.2   Jianhua Xiao, Nankai University
6.3   Jun Liu, Nankai University

Chapter 7   Ling Wang, Nankai University

List of Figures

List of Tables

Environment for the Development of Logistics in China

In 2009, with the international financial crisis lingering and the global economy further declining, China was seriously affected and witnessed its toughest period of economic development since the beginning of the new century. However, the Chinese Government implemented positive financial policies and flexible monetary policies, and gradually improvised a package of plans to deal with the international financial crisis, and so was able to realize an economic recovery ahead of the rest of the world. Meanwhile, the logistics industry was boosted by the issuance of the *Logistics Industry Adjustment and Revitalization Plan*. So far, China's logistics industry has maintained a good development trend.

This chapter gives an overview of the recent developments in China's economic environment and the evolution of its logistics sector, thus laying a foundation for the subsequent chapters. The discussion is anchored in a historical, longitudinal and emerging perspective of the development in the past decades, and brings to light the status of the most recent turbulent two years. Section 1 addresses the overall economic growth, the expanding international trade, the flourishing domestic demand and the Government's mega-stimulus program for the nation's economy. Section 2 provides a comprehensive depiction of the logistics scene, covering the transition of the logistics system, the scope of the logistics market, the policies, regional plans and cooperation in logistics, and the improvements in the logistics information infrastructure and educational programs. The two sections afford a panoramic view of logistics development in China.

1.1 Economic Environment for the Development of Logistics in China

1.1.1 *Rapid Development of Economic Output*

Since China adopted the reform and opening-up policies in 1978, its economy has attained more than 30 years of rapid development. China's GDP was merely 0.36 trillion RMB in 1978 but grew to 25.73 trillion RMB in 2007, climbing by 9.8% annually and nearly 7% higher than the average growth rate of the global economy.[1] Under the impact of the financial crisis, its economic development slowed down in 2008 and 2009, but it still acquired an 8.7% growth rate owing to the economic stimulus plan, as shown in Figure 1.1.

China's rapid economic growth has provided a powerful support for the development of its logistics industry. The output of China's logistics industry has increased rapidly; the average annual growth rate of the total value of products using logistics services in China reached 17.5% during 2000–2008.[2] In 2009, the main logistics indices showed constant growth, while the pace of growth slowed down: the total value of products using logistics services was 96.7 trillion RMB in 2009, a 7.4% increase on a year-on-year basis, but a drop by 12.1% compared to that in 2008. Total logistics costs in 2009 were 6.1 trillion RMB, 7.2% up on a year-on-year basis, but the rate declined by

---

[1] If unspecified, all statistics and conclusions in this report refer to Mainland China, and do not include Hong Kong, Macao and Taiwan; Hong Kong and Taiwan will be described in detail in Chapter 4. Macao will not be described here because of its geographic size and gambling being its main industry, which means logistics only accounts for a limited proportion of its economy.

[2] The total value of products using logistics services equals the total value of products initially entering the logistics field and delivered to or already received by the end-users during a period of time, representing the value of the logistics demand during a certain time.

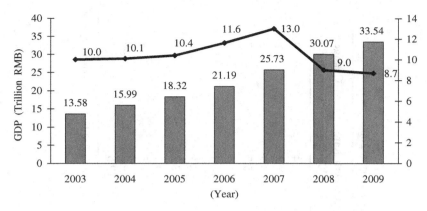

Figure 1.1   China's GDP and Growth Rate for 2003–2009

Source: Compiled from the *China Statistical Yearbook* (2004–2009) and related data in the *2009 China Statistical Bulletin of National Economic and Social Development*, published by the National Bureau of Statistics of China.

Note: Unless otherwise specified, all sources cited in this volume are published in Chinese with referencing information translated into English.

9% compared to 2008.[3] The proportion of logistics costs in GDP was 18.1% in 2009, same as that in 2008. The volume of various means of transport kept increasing in the year, but the rate of growth also declined obviously, as shown in Table 1.1.

1.1.2 *Rapid Expansion of Industrial Scale*

Through 30 years of development, China has established a solid base of industries: industrial added value increased from 0.16 trillion RMB in 1978 to 13.46 trillion RMB in 2009, with an average annual growth rate of 15.9%. Presently, its output of over 100 products in more than 10 industries, such as coal, steel, cement, chemical, building materials, textile, home appliance and electronics, ranks No. 1 in the world. Global industrial clusters for various fields were established, e.g., Zhongshan and Dongguan as the centers for textile and apparel, Foshan and Chaozhou as the centers for ceramics and building materials, Shenzhen

---

[3] Total logistics costs refers to the total spent in the national economy on logistics.

Table 1.1 Total Values and Growth Rates of Various Means of Transport in 2009

Index	Unit	Absolute Value	Growth Rate in 2009 (%)	Growth Rate in 2008 (%)	Change in Growth Rate (%)
Total value of transportation					
Railway	Billion tons	27.9	7.5	9.4	-1.9
Highway	Billion tons	3.3	1.9	4.7	-2.8
Water carriage	Billion tons	21.0	9.4	10.9	-1.5
Civil aviation	Billion tons	3.1	3.0	5.7	-2.7
Pipeline	100,000 tons	44.6	9.3	1.4	7.9
	Billion tons	0.4	1.3	15.4	-14.1
Total freight flows					
Railway	Billion ton-km	12121.1	9.8	3.8	6.0
Highway	Billion ton-km	2523.9	0.5	3.7	-3.2
Water carriage	Billion ton-km	3638.4	10.7	14.5	-3.8
Civil aviation	Billion ton-km	5744.0	14.0	1.5	12.5
Pipeline	Billion ton-km	12.6	5.6	2.8	2.8
	Billion ton-km	202.2	4.1	19.5	-15.4

Source: Compiled from the *2009 China Statistical Bulletin of National Economic and Social Development*, published by the National Bureau of Statistics of China.

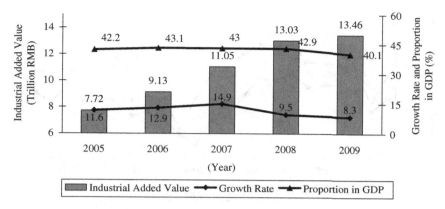

Figure 1.2   Industrial Added Value, Growth Rate and Proportion in GDP for 2005–2009

Source: Compiled from the *China Statistical Yearbook* (2004–2009) and related data in the *2009 China Statistical Bulletin of National Economic and Social Development*, published by the National Bureau of Statistics of China.

and Dongguan as the centers for electronic equipment. As a result, China has become the second largest manufacturing country in the world, after the US. Figure 1.2 shows the industrial added value, its growth rate and proportion in GDP for 2005–2009.

The rapid development of China's industries has elevated its general demand for logistics and has accelerated the development of third-party logistics such as petrochemical logistics, steel logistics, building materials logistics, electronic products logistics and automotive logistics, as well as propelling the growth of logistics parks servicing large-scale manufacturing bases.

1.1.3 *Impact on International Trade*

Because of the impact of the global financial crisis, the import and export value of China's foreign trade has shown a decline since September 2008. Due to the recovery of the global economy, this downward trend in foreign trade was reversed in the second half of 2009. Then the total value of import and export began to increase in November, compared with the same period in 2008, showing a rapid

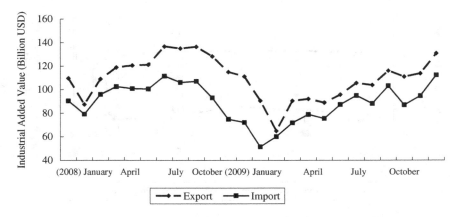

Figure 1.3   Trend of Monthly Import and Export Values for 2008–2009

Source: Related data published by the General Administration of Customs of the People's Republic of China.

recovery in China's foreign trade (Figure 1.3). Although the downward trend of foreign trade changed in 2009, the total value of foreign trade was still lower than that in 2008: the total import and export value in 2009 was 2.21 trillion USD, a negative 13.9% growth compared with that in 2008, and the first-ever negative growth, as shown in Figure 1.4.

The downward trend of international trade severely affected China's international logistics market: total cargo throughput of ports above the designated size[4] in 2009 was 6.9 billion tons, 8.2% up compared with that in 2008, yet the rate of growth declined by 3.3%. Of these values, freight for foreign trade was 2.1 billion tons, 8.6% up compared with that in 2008, and the rate of growth increased by 1.6%; while container throughput at ports was only 120.8 million TEUs (Twenty-Foot Equivalent Units), down by 5.8% compared with that in 2008.[5] The downward trend of international trade had a

---

[4] Ports above the designated size are those sea ports with annual cargo throughput over 1 million tons and inland ports with annual cargo throughput over 2 million tons and ports for international trade, for container load and unload, as specified by the Chinese Ministry of Transport.

[5] *2009 China Statistical Bulletin of National Economic and Social Development*, the National Bureau of Statistics of China, 2010.

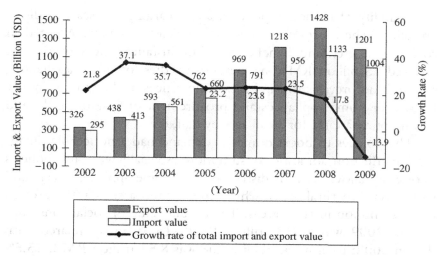

Figure 1.4 Total Import and Export Values and Growth Rates for 2002–2009

Source: Compiled from the *China Statistical Bulletin of National Economic and Social Development* (2002–2009), published by the National Bureau of Statistics of China.

more serious impact on coastal ports that rely more on foreign trade, and all of them suffered negative growth. Cargo throughput at Shenzhen Port was 194 million tons in 2009, 8.3% down compared with that in 2008; its container throughput was 18.3 million TEUs, 14.78% down compared with that in 2008.[6] Container throughput at Shanghai Port was 25 million TEUs in 2009, 10.7% down compared with that in 2008, with growth being negative for the first time.[7]

1.1.4 *Flourishing Demand due to Domestic Consumption*

In 2009, China's Central Government adopted a package of economic policies to stimulate domestic consumption: massively increasing financial expenditures, implementing structural tax-cuts, maintaining the rapid growth of monetary credits, improving the

---

[6] The Transport Commission of Shenzhen Municipality. http://www.sz.gov.cn/jtj/tjsj/zxtjxx.

[7] *2009 China Statistical Bulletin of National Economic and Social Development*, the National Bureau of Statistics of China, 2010.

sustainability of monetary policies, and enlarging the scale of direct financing. These economic incentive policies are unprecedented in coverage, degree and beneficiaries. For instance, the Government invested 45 billion RMB in offering subsidies for home appliances, cars and motorcycles to rural areas, allowances in the trade-in policy for cars or home appliances and procurement of farming tools, and cutting purchase tax for small cars by half, etc.

The policies to boost domestic demand had a noticeable, invigorating effect on domestic consumption, especially with such policies as offering allowances for distribution of home appliances, cars and motorcycles to rural areas, which engendered a substantial growth in consumption in rural areas. Total retail value of social consumption in 2009 was 12.53 trillion RMB, 15.5% up compared with that in 2008; total urban retail value was 8.51 trillion RMB, 15.5% up compared with that in 2008; total rural retail value was 4.02 trillion RMB, 15.7% up, and it was the first time the rural growth rate surpassed that of the urban area. Please see Figure 1.5 for details.

The growth in domestic consumption has pushed the logistics industry to develop prosperously in the domestic market, which thus

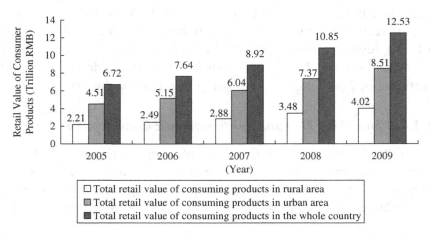

Figure 1.5 Change in Total Retail Value of Social Consumer Products for 2005–2009

Source: Compiled from the *China Statistical Bulletin of National Economic and Social Development* (2005–2009), published by the National Bureau of Statistics of China.

mitigated the impact from the downward trend of the international logistics market. Total logistics value of import and export in 2009 decreased by 12.8% compared with that in 2008; while total logistics values of domestic agricultural products, renewable resources, institutional and residential products increased by 4.3%, 12.3% and 16.4% respectively compared with that in 2008.

1.1.5 *Implementation of the 4 Trillion RMB Incentive Plan*

To counter the impact of the international financial crisis, China implemented an investment plan valued at 4 trillion RMB from 2009 to 2010 to stimulate its economic growth, of which 1.5 trillion RMB was invested in the construction of railways, highways, airports and the national electric grid, accounting for 38% of the total investment amount (Figure 1.6). Hence, the pace of construction of transportation

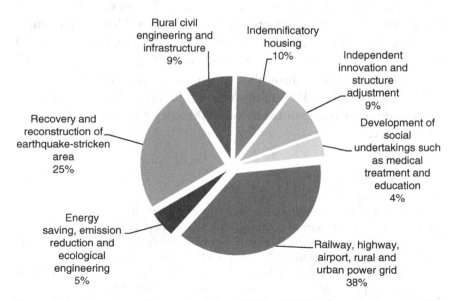

Figure 1.6   Investment Structure of the 4 Trillion RMB Economic Incentive Plan

Source: Compiled from "4 trillion RMB investment program", published by the National Development and Reform Commission of China. http://www.sdpc.gov.cn/xwzx/xwtt/t20090306_264928.htm.

infrastructure was sped up, and the level of infrastructure was upgraded. While improving economic growth directly, this also offset the deficiencies of the transportation infrastructure which had long lagged behind economic development.

In the history of railways in China, the year 2009 ranks highest in the scale and output of investment. Total investment in basic construction in 2009 was 600 billion RMB, 265 billion RMB more (and 79% higher) than that in 2008. This total value of investment in 2009 surpassed the total amount of investment in railway construction for the Ninth Five-Year Plan and the Tenth Five-Year Plan, resulting in 6,000 km of newly added mileage. Its total railway mileage of 86,000 km is the second highest in the world.[8]

Construction of basic infrastructure for railways, waterways and civil aviation has accelerated markedly. Total fixed asset investment in highways, waterways and civil aviation was 1.13 trillion RMB, 31% up compared with that in 2008; the newly added highway mileage was 98,000 km, of which the expressway mileage was 4,720 km. The number of newly added deep-water berths with a capacity of over 10,000 tons was 96, the improved inland waterway mileage was 1,192 km,[9] while the newly added throughput for berths with a capacity of over 10,000 tons was 313.18 million tons.[10] The area of civil airport terminal buildings was expanded by 660,000 m^2; six freight airports were newly added.[11]

---

[8] *2009 Railway Statistics Bulletin*, the Ministry of Railways of China, 2010.

[9] From the speech of Li Shenglin, the Minister of Transport, at the National Working Conference of 2010. http://www.moc.gov.cn/zhuzhan/jiaotongxinwen/xinwenredian/201001xinwen/201001/t20100117_652171.html.

[10] The *2009 Statistical Bulletin of National Economic Development and Social Development of China*, published by the National Bureau of Statistics of China.

[11] "2009, a good year for China's civil aviation", the Civil Aviation Administration of China. http://www.caac.gov.cn/D1/2010GZH/2009HG/201001/t20100118_29744.html.

1.2 Policies and Environment for the Development of China's Logistics Industry

1.2.1 *Breakthrough in the Reformation of the Logistics Management System*

Logistics is a composite industry spanning many government departments and industries, involving various means of transport such as railway, highway, waterway and aviation, and covering many related government departments, e.g., commerce, taxation, foreign trade and information. The Chinese Government has continually improved the management system of and innovated new policies for the logistics industry to prompt its development.

In February 2005, the National Development and Reform Commission (NDRC) issued the *Notice of the National Development and Reform Commission of the PRC on the Establishment of a Joint Conference System for National Modern Logistics*, which marked the initial formation of a coordination mechanism for national modern logistics. The task involved 15 departments and units, such as the NDRC, Ministry of Commerce, Ministry of Railways, Ministry of Communications, Ministry of Information Industry, and was led by the NDRC.

The Ministry of Transport was established in March 2008, integrating the duties of the former Ministry of Communications, the former National Civil Aviation Administration and part of the duties of the former Ministry of Construction in managing urban passenger transport and the State Post Bureau. Given the specific nature of railway construction and management in China, the Ministry of Railways has been retained. The chief duties of the Ministry of Transport include making and implementing plans, policies and standards for the highway, waterway and civil aviation industries, carrying out the programming and coordination for comprehensive transportation systems, and improving the interface among various means of transport. The establishment of the Ministry of Transport has changed the situation where all means of transport were previously segregated, thus signifying a breakthrough in the management system for China's logistics industry.

1.2.2 *Successive Issuance of Logistics Policies*

In recent years, the Government has issued many policies to prompt the development of China's logistics industry, greatly enhancing the status of the logistics industry in the national economy and playing a significant role in promoting its rapid development.

In August 2004, China issued the *Opinions of the State Council on Promoting Modern Logistics in China,* which became the guiding document for the development of logistics in China. The *Outline of the Eleventh Five-Year Plan for National Economic and Social Development* was issued in March 2006, which definitely prompted the full-scale development of the modern logistics industry and elevated the logistics industry to national-level planning. The *Opinions of the State Council Concerning Accelerating the Development of the Service Sector,* issued by the State Council in March 2007, put forward the mandate to enhance the level of specialization and socialization of logistics, to extensively develop the third-party logistics industry, and to deepen the reforms of the railway, civil aviation and other service industries.

To counter the global financial crisis, the State Council issued the *Logistics Industry Adjustment and Revitalization Plan* in March 2009, making the logistics industry the sole service industry program among the revitalization programs for 10 industries. It also placed the development of the logistics industry in the package of plans for countering the international financial crisis, thus elevating the development of the logistics industry to the national strategic level. Subsequently, most provinces in China issued detailed matching plans. In addition, the revised *Postal Law of the PRC* was implemented in October 2009 to regulate the courier market with laws and regulations. Table 1.2 lists the main policies issued on logistics in China in recent years.

1.2.3 *Continual Enlargement of Logistics Market*

Along with the reform and opening-up of China's economy, the degree of openness of the logistics market has increased constantly.

Table 1.2 Partial Outline of China's Logistics Policies

Date of Issuance	Policy
2004–06	*Outline of the Reform and Development of the Circulation Industry*
2004–08	*Opinions of the State Council on Promoting Modern Logistics in China*
2007–01	*Measures for the Administration of Food Safety in the Circulation Sector*
2007–03	*Opinions of the State Council Concerning Accelerating the Development of the Service Sector*
2007–07	*National Plan for Inland Waterways and Ports*
2007–07	*National Plan for Coastal Port Layout*
2007–08	*National Plan for Highway Transport Hub Layout*
2007–08	*Development Plan for Modern Grain Logistics*
2007–10	*Medium- and Long-Range Development Plan for Comprehensive Transportation Network*
2007–11	*Opinions of the State Council on Promoting a Sound and Rapid Development of Modern Transportation*
2007–12	*Opinions of the State Council Concerning Accelerating the Development of Modern Transportation*
2008–01	*National Plan for Civil Airport Layout*
2008–07	*Measures for the Administration of Express Delivery Business Market*
2008–10	*Medium- and Long-Range Plan for Railway Network (amended in 2008)*
2008–12	*Opinions of the State Council on the Invigoration of Circulation and Expansion of Consumption*
2008–12	*Notice of the State Council on Implementing the Price and Tax Reform of Refined Oil*
2009–03	*Logistics Industry Adjustment and Revitalization Plan*
2009–04	*Postal Law of the People's Republic of China*
2009–09	*Measures for the Administration of Express Delivery Business Permits*
2009–11	*Notice on Strengthening the Administration of Circulation of Pharmaceuticals*

Pursuant to its promises upon entering the WTO, starting from December 11, 2004, China annulled the limits on foreign investment concerning region and proportion of shares in many industries such as highway cargo transportation and cargo leasing, while business areas involving logistics were opened up completely. The details are listed in Table 1.3. Currently, foreign capital enters various areas of

Table 1.3   Clauses Pertaining to Logistics in Sino-US WTO Agreement

Area	Main Content and Opening Time
Highway cargo transportation	Foreign businessmen are permitted to operate joint-venture enterprises by means of shareholding within one year of China entering the WTO, and are permitted to become sole proprietors within three years of China entering the WTO.
Railway transportation	Starting from 2002, foreign businessmen are permitted to operate joint-venture enterprises by means of shareholding within three years of China entering the WTO, and permitted to become sole proprietors within six years.
Storage industry	Starting from 2002, foreign businessmen are permitted to operate joint-venture enterprises by means of shareholding within one year of China entering the WTO, and permitted to become sole proprietors within three years.
Freight agency	Starting from 2002, foreign businessmen are permitted to operate joint-venture enterprises by means of owning 50% of shares after China enters the WTO, permitted to operate joint-venture enterprises by means of shareholding within one year of China entering the WTO, and permitted to become sole proprietors within four years.
Container station operator	Starting from 2002, foreign businessmen are permitted to operate joint-venture enterprises after China enters the WTO.
Cargo loading and unloading, customs clearance and shipping agency	Starting from 2002, foreign businessmen are permitted to operate joint-venture enterprises after China enters the WTO.

Source: "A study of the impact and policies of China's entry into the WTO on transportation management of Shanghai city", published by the Shanghai Municipal Transport and Port Authority.

logistics in China, mainly the following: international cargo transportation, courier service in particular; port logistics, such as opening container liner routes; production and supply of logistics equipment and facilities; training of logistics talents; software for logistics information platforms; logistics real estate, especially in port construction.

1.2.4 *Successive Issuance of National-Level Regional Plans*

In 2009, China achieved great progress in its regional coordinative development. China's State Council successively issued 11 regional revitalizing plans such as *Opinions on Supporting Fujian Province to Accelerate the Construction of the Taiwan Strait West Coast Economic Zone*. The number of plans issued, as seen in Figure 1.7, is almost the

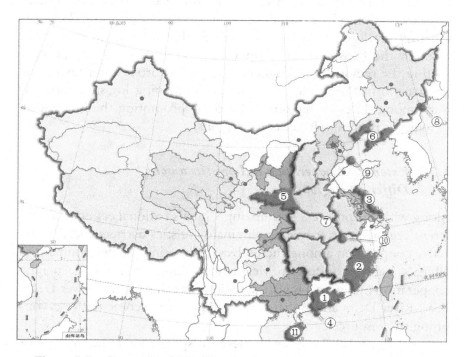

Figure 1.7   Geographical Map Showing Spread of 11 National-Level Plans

Note: The numbered regional plans in the figure are ordered according to their time of issuance: (1) *Plan Outline for the Reform and Development of the Pearl River Delta*; (2) *Opinions on Supporting Fujian Province to Accelerate the Construction of the Taiwan Strait West Coast Economic Zone*; (3) *Development Plan for Jiangsu Coastal Region*; (4) *Overall Development Plan for Hengqin*; (5) *Development Plan for Guanzhong-Tianshui Economic Zone*; (6) *Development Plan for Liaoning Coastal Economic Zone*; (7) *Development Plan for the Central Region*; (8) *Plan Outline for the Cooperative Development of the Tumen River Area*; (9) *Development Plan for the High-efficiency Ecological Economic Zone of the Yellow River Delta*; (10) *Plan for the Ecological Economic Zone of Panyang Lake*; (11) *Views on Promoting the Development of Hainan International Tourism Island*.

sum total of those issued in the previous four years. Here, construction of logistics infrastructure was the key item among many plans, namely, the construction of modern and comprehensive transportation systems for the Pearl River Delta, Western Taiwan Straits Economic Zone, Central Region, and Guanzhong-Tianshui Economic Zone; ports in Jiangsu Coastal Region; the shipping center in Liaoning Coastal Economic Zone; the international logistics base in the Tumen River Area facing Northeast Asia. Planning and implementation of regional development helps to promote the coordinative development of regions and further develop more regions through the construction of important projects, especially by promoting the regional development of logistics through improving the construction of logistics infrastructure, deepening logistics cooperation among different regions and actively promoting the integration of logistics resources in different regions.

1.2.5 *Extensive Cooperation in Logistics among Different Regions*

Along with the progress in unitizing China's regional economies, different regions have striven to eliminate logistics barriers and develop active cooperation among themselves, promoting the development of China's logistics industry. Meanwhile, along with the deepening cooperation in regional logistics, regions like the Yangtze River Delta, Pearl River Delta and Bohai Rim Region have become the reservoirs of logistic resources.

In August 2007, a joint conference system for modern logistics was established in the Yangtze River Delta, marking a significant stage of development for logistics cooperation in the Yangtze River Delta. In June 2009, Jiangsu Province, Zhejiang Province and Shanghai City (the "two provinces plus one city") jointly issued the *Opinions on Promoting the Integration of Highway Freight (Logistics) in the Yangtze River Delta*, to foster barrier-free movement of logistics factors in the Yangtze River Delta and promote the integration of highway freight (logistics) in the area. In addition, the area began innovating regional passage models, gradually realizing communication and information sharing among the two provinces plus one city through the establishment of an electronic platform for ports in the Delta.

Cooperation in logistics in the Pearl River Delta is mainly manifested in the linkage and coordination of transportation infrastructure. In June 2004, the *Pan-Pearl River Delta Regional Cooperation Framework Agreement* was signed officially — nine collaborative networks would be established in the Pan-Pearl River Delta, including the Regional Transportation Fast Network and the Regional Information Communication Network. Currently, the Pearl River Delta has formed a port cluster with a system of division of labor: Hong Kong as the center of international freight and Guangzhou-Shenzhen as the main hubs. The Hong Kong–Zhuhai–Macao Bridge and other highway infrastructures are also under active construction now.

In April 2006, the *Tianjin Proposal on Promoting Regional Cooperation in the Bohai Rim Region* was signed, pointing out that improving cooperation in regional logistics is the key to speeding up economic cooperation in the Bohai Rim Region. Currently, a cooperative transportation platform and a logistics network are being established in Beijing, Tianjin and Hebei Province, focusing mainly on coordinating and unifying customs clearance and related policies.

Meanwhile, logistics cooperation is being deepened among Mainland China, Taiwan and Hong Kong. The Central Government, Hong Kong and Macao signed and began implementing the *Closer Economic Partnership Arrangement between the Mainland and Hong Kong* (CEPA) on January 1, 2004, opening the Mainland logistics market to Hong Kong and Macao. In May 2009, *Supplement 6 to the Closer Economic Partnership Arrangement between the Mainland and Hong Kong* (CEPA6) was signed in Hong Kong, increasing the areas of trade in Mainland open to Hong Kong from 40 to 42.

In November 2008, four agreements addressing direct transport, direct post and direct trade were signed between the Mainland and Taiwan to actualize the "three directs". In June 2010, the *Economic Cooperation Framework Agreement between the Mainland and Taiwan* (ECFA) was signed to further develop the direct air transport business.

1.2.6 *Steady Progress in Standardization and Informatization*

Logistics development in China had previously been hampered by non-standardization and an inferior level of informatization. Following years of gradual progress, logistics in China has gained some ground in standardization and informatization.

In September 2003, the National Logistics Standardization Technical Committee and China Logistics Information Standardization Technical Committee were successively established. In May 2007, the *Logistics Terms* and the *Calculation and Evaluation of Enterprise Logistics Cost*, two fundamental national standards in logistics were implemented. In October 2007, standards for logistics parks and pallet logistics were formulated. By September 2008, the number of national logistics standards and professional standards completed, being compiled and in the planning stage had reached 110. In November 2009, the National Standards Committee completed the *Special Plan of 2009–2011 for National Logistics Standards*, putting forward 150 national standards and professional standards in 13 important fields needing revision within three years.

In terms of logistics informatization, Shanghai Sub-center, the first sub-center of China E-Port Data Center, was formally established in May 2002, marking the beginning of the construction of an information platform for public logistics. Currently, the *Guiding Opinions on Accelerating the Construction of the National and Regional Public Information Platforms for Modern Logistics*, aiming to speed up the construction of national-level and regional-level information platforms for logistics, is being compiled; Beijing, Shanghai and Zhejiang Province have been successful in the construction of public logistics information platforms. In 2010, the *Development Plan for Logistics Informatization (2010–2015)* was compiled by the Ministry of Industry and Information Technology, specifically listing the goals and main tasks of promoting the development of logistics informatization and organizing the pilot work of logistics informatization.

1.2.7 *Gradual Improvement of Logistics Education*

In the recent decade, China's logistics education system has improved along with the gradual increase in scale of logistics education. Since the logistics management major was established in 2000, the number of universities registered with or approved by the Ministry of Education to offer an undergraduate major in logistics increased from 1 in 2000 to 338 in 2009. Please see Figure 1.8 for the growth trend. China has gradually established a multi-level logistics education system including professional education, undergraduate education and postgraduate education, resulting in a continuous improvement in the overall level of logistics education.

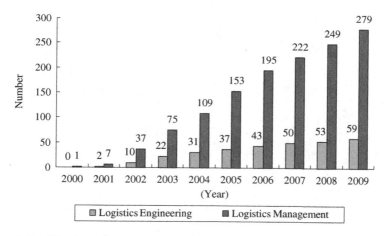

Figure 1.8   Number of Universities Registered with or Approved by the Ministry of Education to Offer Undergraduate Major in Logistics for 2000–2009

Source: "List of Undergraduate Majors for Universities Registered with or Approved by the Ministry of Education" (2000–2009), published by the Ministry of Education of China.

Development Status of China's Logistics Market

In 2009, China witnessed the slowing down of the prior rapid growth in its logistics market under the impact of the global financial crisis and a set of anti-crisis policies adopted by the Chinese Government. The demand for logistics in the international market remained depressed while the demand in the domestic market remained stable, with rapid growth in cars, home appliances and some other hot markets. For market supply, the influences of slowing growth on demand and increasing costs on operations resulted in the poor performance of many logistics enterprises; some local logistics enterprises began to actively merge with other enterprises, while foreign-funded enterprises rapidly entered China's diversified emerging market.

This chapter begins with the overall scale of China's logistics expenses for the most recent years, the logistics market and the various demand sectors after the international financial crisis. It then gives an analytical exposition of the logistics enterprises, in terms of performance, transformation, foreign competition and the financial resources for growth. Up-to-date statistics are provided for a more concrete understanding of the logistics market in China.

2.1 Overall Scale of Market

From 2000 to 2007, the overall development of China's logistics market has shown swift growth with rapid enlargement of the market due to continual and brisk development of the Chinese economy. But after 2008, the pace of growth of China's logistics market has slowed down due to the impact of the global financial crisis on China's economy.

2.1.1 *Total Value of Social Logistics*

The total value of social logistics in 2009 was 96.7 trillion RMB, 7.4% up from that in 2008; but the rate of growth decreased by 12.1 and 18.8 percentage points compared with 2008 and 2007, respectively. In addition, 2009 was the only year since 2000 with a growth rate lower than 10% (as shown in Figure 2.1).

2.1.2 *Total Expenses of Social Logistics*

In 2009, the total expenses of social logistics in China was 6.08 trillion RMB, 7.2% up compared with that in 2008 (as seen in Table 2.1), accounting for 18.1% of GDP, the same percentage as that in 2008.

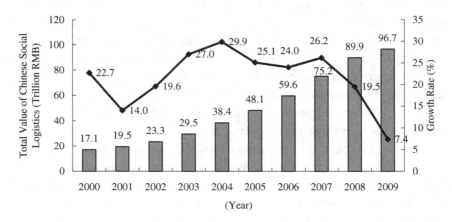

Figure 2.1   Total Value of China's Social Logistics and Growth Rate for 2000–2009

Source: Compiled from (i) *Logistics Condition Analysis of the First Half of 2005*, published by the China Federation of Logistics and Purchasing and the China Logistics Information Centre, and (ii) related data in the *National Logistics Report* (2005–2009) published by the National Development and Reform Commission, the National Bureau of Statistics in China and the China Federation of Logistics and Purchasing.

Table 2.1   Total Expenses of and Growth Rate of Social Logistics in China for 2005–2009

Year	Total Expenses of Logistics (Trillion RMB)	Growth Rate (%)	Share in GDP (%)
2005	3.39	12.9	18.6
2006	3.84	13.5	18.3
2007	4.54	18.2	18.4
2008	5.45	16.2	18.1
2009	6.08	7.2	18.1

Source: Data from the *National Logistics Report* (2005–2009), published by the National Development and Reform Commission, the National Bureau of Statistics of China and the China Federation of Logistics and Purchasing.

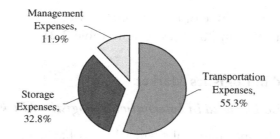

Figure 2.2   Composition of Total Expenses of Social Logistics in China for 2009

Source: Data from the *National Logistics Report* (2005–2009), published by the National Development and Reform Commission, the National Bureau of Statistics of China and the China Federation of Logistics and Purchasing.

In 2009, transportation expenses were 3.36 trillion RMB, accounting for 55.3% of the total expenses of logistics; storage or holding expenses were 2 trillion RMB, accounting for 32.8%; and management expenses were 0.72 trillion RMB, accounting for 11.9% (Figure 2.2).

2.1.3 *Added Value of Logistics Industry in China*

In 2009, the added value of the logistics industry in China was 2.31 trillion RMB, 7.3% up compared with that in 2008; it accounted for

Table 2.2   Added Value of China's Logistics Industry and Growth Rate for 2005–2009

Year	Added Value of Logistics (Trillion RMB)	Growth Rate (%)	Share in Service Industry (%)
2005	1.21	12.7	16.6
2006	1.41	15.1	17.1
2007	1.70	20.3	17.6
2008	2.00	15.4	16.5
2009	2.31	7.3	16.1

Source: Data from the *National Logistics Report* (2005–2009), published by the National Development and Reform Commission, the National Bureau of Statistics of China and the China Federation of Logistics and Purchasing.

16.1% of the added value of the national service industry, 0.4% down compared with that in 2008 (as seen in Table 2.2).

2.2   Demand in Logistics Market

2.2.1   *Sluggish Demand in International Logistics Market*

Since 2008, the international financial crisis has depressed the consumption demand of China's key export destinations, severely affecting China's foreign trade and impinging on China's international logistics demand. Statistics published by China Customs showed that both imports and exports suffered negative growth in November and December of 2008, which were the months most seriously affected by the crisis. The total value of imports and exports in 2009 was 13.9% lower than that in 2008; the actual price-adjusted export value in 2009 decreased by 10.5% while that of imports increased by 1.5%.[1]

The impact of the international financial crisis on the demand in China's international logistics market was also directly reflected by the

---

[1] Data from the General Administration of Customs of the People's Republic of China.

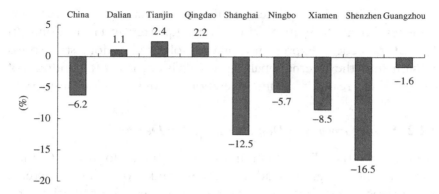

Figure 2.3   Change in Container Throughput at China's Main Coastal Ports in January–November 2009 Compared with the Same Period in 2008

Source: Compiled from data published by the Ministry of Transport of the People's Republic of China.

http://www.moc.gov.cn/zhuzhan/tongjixinxi/tongjishuju/gangkouhuowu_LKTTL/200912/t20091214_643229.html.

container throughput at coastal ports. Figure 2.3 shows that under the impact of the substantial decrease in exports, China's main coastal ports witnessed negative growth in the majority of cities in terms of container throughput except for Dalian, Tianjin and Qingdao which had a small increase in January–November 2009. Moreover, the ports of Shanghai, Shenzhen and other cities which depend heavily on foreign trade all saw a sizable drop in volume.

Many of China's local logistics enterprises, whose main business was in providing import/export logistics services, had poor performance due to insufficient international logistics demand and depressed service prices. For example, in 2009, COSCO lost 7.54 billion RMB and CSCL lost 6.49 billion RMB; the net profit of SINOTRANS in 2009 decreased by 25% compared with that in 2008.

Foreign logistics enterprises engaged in import/export logistics services in China were also affected. Some readjusted their business in China in order to curtail costs and counter the crisis. For example, at the beginning of 2009, Maersk integrated its six regional branches in Qingdao, Shanghai, Xiamen, Guangzhou, Shenzhen and Hong Kong into three branches in Qingdao, Shanghai and Hong Kong, and it closed its China headquarters in Beijing, managing the three new branches directly from its North Asia headquarters in Hong Kong. In April 2009, Federal Express in China consolidated its domestic express division into the international express division, laid off hundreds of sales staff and readjusted some operation stations with less business.

2.2.2 *Stable Growth in Domestic Logistics Demand*

Contrary to the dire situation of international logistics, China's domestic logistics grew steadily in 2009 thanks to the rapid increase in domestic investment and consumption under the promotion of a package of policies adopted by the Government to boost domestic demand. The total investment in social fixed assets in 2009 increased by 33.3% compared with that in 2008, making it the year with the fastest increase since 1981; the total retail value of social consumption in 2009 increased by 16.9% compared with that in 2008, making it the year with the fastest increase since 1986. The growth rates of social investment and final consumption accounted respectively for 8% and 4.6% in the growth rate of GDP, stably promoting the increase in domestic logistics demand and being the main driving force behind the increase in China's logistics demand in 2009.

For example, from January to November 2009, container through-put at Chinese inland ports, with an annual container throughput of more than 10 million tons, increased by 8.8% compared with the same period in 2008 (exceeding the national growth rate of 8%), due to the relatively small impact of foreign trade on them. In 2009, the total cargo throughput of all airports in China was 9.46 million tons; of that, the cargo throughput of domestic airlines increased by 10.85% compared with that in 2008. The proportion in total cargo throughput increased from 63.8% in 2008 to 66.1% in 2009, which was in sharp contrast with the growth rate of 0.32% for international airlines.

2.2.3 *Flourishing Demand in Hot Market Segments*

In 2009, in order to counter the negative impact of the financial crisis and ensure stable economic development, the Chinese Government adopted a package of measures to stimulate domestic consumption, of which the car, home appliances and network-shopping markets became the biggest beneficiaries and saw a big increase in sales. Naturally these market segments became the highlights for logistics demand in the domestic market that year.

Automobiles

Following the rapid development of the Chinese economy in the recent three decades, the income of citizens has been substantially raised; many families have attained the financial means to purchase a car. Therefore China became the country with the fastest increase in demand for cars in the world. In 2009, the Government put forward a set of incentive plans on car consumption to further speed up the pace of families acquiring cars. Statistics from the China Association of Automobile Manufacturers showed that the total number of cars produced in 2009 was 13.79 million, 48.3% up compared with that in 2008; sales of cars was 13.64 million in that year, 46.2% up compared with that in 2008.

The business and income of some enterprises engaging in automotive logistics saw a robust increase due to the rapid growth in the production and sales of cars. For example, merely between January and July 2009, the business of Beijing Changjiu Logistics Co., Ltd. increased by 70% compared with that in 2008; the company delivered more than 80,000 cars in July 2009 alone, while the figure was only 30,000 cars in the same month in 2008. The business of Anji Automotive Logistics Co., Ltd. in 2009 increased by 30%, with delivery climbing to three million cars that year. The income of Chongqing Changan Minsheng Logistics Co., Ltd. for the first three quarters of 2009 was 1.03 billion RMB, 42.7% up compared with that in 2008.

Home appliances

In 2009, the Government subsidized urban and rural citizens to buy new home appliances, effectively stimulating the production and sales of home appliances. China produced 99 million color televisions in

2009, 9.6% up compared with that in 2008; the output of home refrigerators was 59 million, 24.7% up compared with that in 2008.

Rural regions became the main source of increase in home appliance sales in 2009, due to the already high ownership of home appliances among urban families. Currently, the logistics system in rural regions still lags behind that in urban regions; the majority of deliveries of products are provided by retailers and the minority by home appliance manufacturers and logistics enterprises. For example, Haier Group, one of the home appliance manufacturers, emphasizes the establishment of a delivery network in rural regions. It has gained the favor of rural consumers, with a market share of over one third in rural products, due to its far-reaching delivery service in rural regions and fast delivery to consumers. China Post Logistics, as a state-owned logistics enterprise under China Post Group, has gained a share of the rural delivery market because of its widespread coverage in rural regions derived from its extensive postal network.

Network shopping

Along with the gradual improvement of China's e-business laws and technological environment, as well as the change in the citizens' mode of consumption, China's network-shopping market in 2009, especially the B2C and C2C markets which deal with individual consumers, entered a stage of rapid development. Statistics from iResearch showed that the transaction value of China's network-shopping market in 2009 was 248.35 billion RMB, 93.7% up compared with that in 2008; the business of B2B operators increased by 20%, similar to the growth rate in 2008; the scale of the C2C market in 2009 increased by 100% compared with that in 2008; the size of the B2C market in 2009 increased by more than 200% compared with that in 2008, representing the fastest increase in scale.

Propelled by the rapidly developing B2C and C2C network-shopping markets, the demand for delivery services has increased greatly. Taobao Network, a major C2C e-business platform in China, handled 2 million orders in daily transactions in 2008; this number had climbed to 3 million orders per day by June 2009. Assuming that

75% of ordered products needed delivery, Taobao Network would have delivered more than 600 million packages in 2009.

The rapid increase in the logistics demand from the B2C and C2C network-shopping markets led to the quick growth of domestic courier enterprises in China. In 2009, domestic courier enterprises delivered 186 million packages, 22.8% up compared with that in 2008; their total income was 47.9 billion RMB, 17.3% up compared with that in 2008.

2.3 Logistics Enterprises

2.3.1 *Poor Performance of Enterprises*

Due to factors such as sluggish demand, decreasing service prices and increase in fuel prices, tax and labor costs, China's domestic logistics enterprises experienced greater operational pressures in 2009 than in 2008, with the majority performing poorly.

Statistics from the China Federation of Logistics and Purchasing on key domestic logistics enterprises show that the main business indices of key enterprises generally declined during the first three quarters in 2009. For example, cargo transportation, delivery and logistics processing decreased by 1.5%, 17.3% and 16.5% respectively compared with that in the same period in 2008. Meantime, about 60% of the surveyed enterprises showed a negative growth in profit compared with that in 2008, while 17% of the surveyed enterprises showed a loss.

Statistics from the China Materials Storage and Transportation Association on 61 large-scale storage enterprises nationwide showed that the cargo throughput of these enterprises was 80.19 million tons in 2009, only 0.4% up compared with that in 2008; the income of the main business of these enterprises was 18 billion RMB in 2009, 11% down compared with that in 2008.

2.3.2 *Mergers and Acquisitions Carried Out by Local Enterprises*

Many mergers and acquisitions took place in China's logistics market from 2005 to 2008. In most cases, foreign logistics enterprises carried

Table 2.3   Main Mergers and Acquisitions in China's Logistics Market for 2005–2008

Acquirer	Transferor	Type of Transferor	Year
Dutch TNT	Arima	Less-than-carload lot carrier	2005
FedEx	Daejeon	Express delivery enterprise	2006
Schneider	Po Wan	Comprehensive logistics	2007
YRC Logistics	Jia Yu	Less-than-carload lot carrier	2008

Source: Yu Xingyuan *et al.*, "Pattern analysis and policies of foreign investment entering into logistics market of China", *Comprehensive Transport*, 2009(3): 44–48.

out mergers and acquisitions with local enterprises in China in order to rapidly deploy their markets in China (see Table 2.3). In 2009, mergers and acquisitions had a different nature, taking place among local larger-scale Chinese enterprises, with the purposes of improving services, sharing resources and strengthening cooperation.

For example, China National Foreign Trade Transportation (Group) Corporation and China Changjiang National Shipping (Group) Corporation were merged into SINOTRANS in March 2009. The core business of SINOTRANS, after the merger, focuses on logistics, freight forwarding and marine shipping, while the original Changjiang National Shipping (Group) still focuses its business on shipping along the Yangtze River; so the merger is helpful for complementing mutual advantages and improving the logistics service chain.

China Express Delivery Service Company of China Post Group and China Post Logistics Co., Ltd. were merged into China Post Express Delivery Logistics Company in June 2009. The integration of these two large companies mainly concerns the management system of express delivery logistics, business products and client resources, to implement a unified operational model for integrating sales, storage and delivery, so as to provide clients with international, domestic and local express delivery, unified logistics, storage and delivery, and international package delivery. The merger is helpful as it allows both companies to share resources in space and equipment within the same city, to provide clients with express delivery and logistics services, decrease costs, and improve their services.

In December 2009, New Times International Transport Service Co., Ltd., one of the leading enterprises in international freight forwarding in China, finished the acquisition of Tong Cheng Logistics Group, one of the largest carriers in domestic less-than-carload freight and package delivery. Through this acquisition, New Times expanded its business into domestic highway transportation, integrated international freight forwarding, domestic transportation and third-party logistics, and became the largest comprehensive private logistics enterprise in China.

In addition, many national highway transportation enterprises and port enterprises were re-organized and integrated, to leverage their advantages and improve competitiveness through better division of labor and cooperation.

2.3.3 *Entry of Foreign Enterprises into Emerging Market Segments*

In recent years, along with the citizens' increased income and changing lifestyle, China's emerging market segments such as the cold chain for food and medicine as well as urban express delivery have experienced a noticeable increase in demand, gradual enlargement of market size and higher profits. So, many foreign-funded logistics enterprises began to enter the market, while local logistics enterprises still could not compete with them in terms of funds, technology and management.

In June 2009, DHL established a life science and health care logistics center in Shanghai, engaging mainly in medicine logistics including international air express and shipping, storage and domestic delivery of medicines. In addition, DHL plans to strengthen the refrigeration capacity of its branches in other cities, to increase cold storage with a greater temperature control range and finer classification, as well as to establish a similar logistics center in the northern region of China.

In 2007, logistics group Eimskip entered the logistics field of exporting cold stored food after World Courier entered the cold storage chain of medicine and reagents in China. In 2008, the Australia Swire Group entered the cold storage chain of middle-to-high-end imported food in China. In July 2009, Preferred Freezer Services, the largest logistics supplier of public cold storage in North America, began to build a cold storage of more than 26,000 m^2 in Shanghai, which is one of the largest in scale and most advanced cold storages in China, to provide clients with overall service. Preferred Freezer Services plans to set up a comprehensive modern cold storage network at strategic ports in China in upcoming years, to provide domestic and international food enterprises with good-quality cold storage solutions.

In August 2009, Yamato Logistics Co., Ltd., the largest logistics group in Japan, and Shanghai Bus Logistics Co. established a joint venture company, Yamato (China) Transportation Co., Ltd., aiming to serve the B2C and C2C market segments in network shopping, catalog sales and television shopping. Unlike the ordinary express delivery companies in China, Yamato (China) Transportation customizes its service per client's specifications to take on delivery by time blocks, same-day multiple deliveries and delivery of cold stored goods. It plans to set up a dispatching center with a handling capacity of 1 million transactions per day, having 25 delivery stations and 280 delivery network nodes, and equipped with over 26,000 delivery trucks with cold storage function. Within five years, the annual handling capacity could reach 300 million orders, and the total revenue could top 3 billion RMB.

2.3.4 *Financing Channels for Domestic Medium-Sized and Small Enterprises*

Medium-sized and small logistics enterprises have been constrained by limited financing channels for a long time, due to the underdeveloped financing system in China. Banks, as the main financing source for medium-sized and small logistics firms, most often grant loans based on fixed assets, so that logistics enterprises holding current assets find it difficult to acquire loans. The serious shortage of funds hinders the development of these enterprises. In recent years, this situation has improved along with the development of the financial market in China.

First, some qualified enterprises have acquired investment funds from venture capital. In 2007, Rongqing Group in food cold storage and Jiu Zhoutong Company in medicine logistics respectively attracted 200 million USD and 60 million USD in venture capital. In 2009, Yuan Cheng Group also obtained financial support from China Guangda Investment Management Co., Ltd.

Second, China's capital market launched the Growth Enterprise Market Board financing program to provide innovative medium-sized and small logistics enterprises with new financing channels; Jiangsu Xinning Modern Logistics Co., Ltd., as a listed company, is a case in point. The company's core business is bonded storage and it mainly provides comprehensive third-party logistics services for the material supply, purchasing and production segments in the electronic infor-mation industry supply chain. The IPO of the company raised a capital of 234 million RMB, which will be used in the construction of bonded warehouses and supply chain projects. Upon completion, it will increase the bonded warehouse areas and optimize its network layout to effectively strengthen the company's competitiveness.

The Leap in Infrastructure Development

During the 30 years in which China implemented its reform and opening-up policies, the Chinese Government always emphasized the construction of infrastructure, the majority of which being related to logistics. This not only increased the demand in the domestic market, but also fundamentally changed the conditions in urban and rural areas. In 2009, while the international financial crisis was spreading, the Chinese Government further increased the construction of infrastructure, setting new records for the scale of investment in many fields. The construction of logistics infrastructure in terms of highways, waterways, railways, civil aviation, ports and communication was further increased.

This chapter describes the recent rapid growth of logistics infrastructure in China. Detailed data are synthesized to provide useful statistics on the investment in and construction of physical infrastructure of highways, railways, airports, seaports, inland waterways, logistics parks, dry ports and their capacities. Attention is also given to the status of the supporting information infrastructure.

3.1 Railways and High-Speed Rail

3.1.1 *Investment in Fixed Assets*

From 2005 to 2009, China maintained a high growth rate in the investment in fixed assets of railways. In 2009, China made the largest

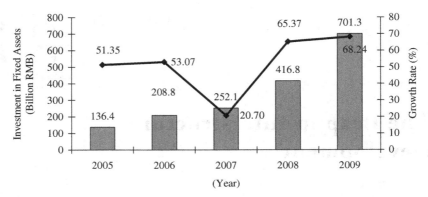

Figure 3.1 Total Investment in Fixed Assets and Growth Rate of Chinese Railway Industry for 2005–2009

Source: Compiled from the *Railway Statistical Bulletin* (2005–2009), published by the Ministry of Railways of China.

investment in railways in history, totaling 701.3 billion RMB in fixed assets, 68.24% up compared with that in 2008 (as seen in Figure 3.1). The amount includes 600.6 billion RMB in the basic construction of railways, a 77.9% increase compared with that in 2008, and 22.7 billion RMB in renovation projects, a 10.4% growth compared with that in 2008.

3.1.2 Development Status of Railway Network

With the continual increase in investments in railway infrastructure in China, the scale of its railway network has grown rapidly. In 2009, China completed building the largest number of new railway lines in its history, with 5,557.3 km of new lines, 4,128.8 km of double-track lines[1] and 8,448.3 km of electrical railway,[2] which increased by 2.2 times, 1.1 times and 3.3 times, respectively, compared with those in 2008. By the end of 2009, China's railway network density had

---

[1] Separate forward and backward bi-directional tracks.

[2] Chinese trains are divided into combustion-engine-based trains and electromotor-based trains; the latter is called the electric railway which has such characteristics as strong power, fast speed, low energy consumption and high efficiency.

Table 3.1   Mileage of China's Railways in Service, 2009

Item	Unit	Value	Growth Rate (%)
Mileage in service	1,000 km	86	7.3
Double-track mileage	1,000 km	33	15.0
Proportion of double-track lines	%	38.8	2.6
Electrical mileage	1,000 km	36	29.4
Proportion of electrical lines	%	41.7	7.1

Source: Compiled from the *Railway Statistical Bulletin* (2009), published by the Ministry of Railways of China.

reached 89.1 km/10,000 km^2, increasing by 6.1 km/10,000 km^2 compared with that in 2008.

Upon the completion of some new railway lines and renovation projects, China's rail network structure improved noticeably. By 2009, there were 33,000 km of double-track lines, equaling a 38.8% rate, 2.6% higher than that in 2008; 36,000 km of electrical lines, amounting to a 41.7% rate, 7.1% up from that in 2008, as shown in Table 3.1.

3.1.3 *Operating Mileage and Freight Volume*

From 2005 to 2009, the railway operating mileage and freight volume maintained a rapid increase in China. In 2009, China's total railway operating mileage reached 86,000 km — a mileage ranking No. 2 in the world, behind the US and followed by Russia. Freight volume in 2009 still increased compared with that in 2008, reaching 3.33 billion tons, as seen in Table 3.2. Meanwhile, along with a bigger investment by the Ministry of Railways in railway construction in the western part of the country, China achieved significant progress and marked results in the construction of railways in the Western region, with the operating mileage reaching 33,000 km, accounting for 38.4% of the total mileage of railways in service, increasing by 2,707 km and 9.2% up from that in 2008.[3]

---

[3] Compiled from the *Railway Statistical Bulletin* (2009), published by the Ministry of Railways of China, 2010.

Table 3.2   Railway Operations in China for 2005 to 2009

Item	Unit	2005	2006	2007	2008	2009
Mileage in service	1,000 km	75	77	78	80	86
Passenger volume	Million	1,156	1,257	1,357	1,462	1,520
Freight volume	Million tons	2,693	2,882	3,142	3,304	3,330

Source: Compiled from the *China Statistical Yearbook* (2009), published by the National Bureau of Statistics of China; and the *Railway Statistical Bulletin* (2009), published by the Ministry of Railways of China.

3.1.4 *Development of High-Speed Passenger Railway*

China achieved swift development in high-speed railway from 2008 to 2009. On August 1, 2008, China's first high-speed railway, the Beijing-Tianjin Intercity Railway, with a speed of over 300 km/h, began operation; on December 26, 2009, the Wuhan-Guangzhou Passenger Special Line, the world's fastest high-speed railway, was launched. By 2009, the mileage of high-speed railways in service reached 6,552 km in China, ranking No. 1 in the world; included in this are 3,676 km of high-speed railway with a speed of 200–350 km/h.

Currently, high-speed railway in China consists of mainly intercity passenger railway, e.g., Beijing-Tianjin, Nanchang-Jiujiang, Wuhan-Guangzhou and Beijing-Shanghai. According to the *Mid- and Long-term Railway Development Plan* published by the Government in 2008, China will build high-speed passenger railways among capital cities and among large and medium metropolises running in four horizontal directions and four vertical directions, as depicted in Figure 3.2. At least 16,000 km of special passenger lines with a speed of over 200 km/h will be set up within the time period.

The development of high-speed passenger railway in China promotes the separation of passenger and cargo transportation lines, which is helpful for developing specialized freight logistics, mitigating the competition between passenger and freight rail lines, thus enhancing the efficiency of freight logistics in deploying, loading/unloading, packing and linking/connecting operations.

Figure 3.2   The "4 Horizontal Directions and 4 Vertical Directions" Schema of China's Railway Passenger Lines

Note: The "4 Vertical Directions" passenger special lines are (1) Beijing-Shanghai; (2) Beijing-Wuhan-Guangzhou-Shenzhen-Hong Kong; (3) Beijing-Shenyang-Harbin; (4) Hangzhou-Ningbo-Fuzhou-Shenzhen. The "4 Horizontal Directions" passenger special lines are (1) Xuzhou-Zhengzhou-Lanzhou; (2) Hangzhou-Nanchang-Changsha-Kunming; (3) Qingdao-Shijiazhuang-Taiyuan; (4) Shanghai-Nanjing-Wuhan-Chongqing-Chengdu.

Source: Compiled from the *Railway Statistical Bulletin* (2009), published by the Ministry of Railways of China.

3.1.5 *Energy Consumption and Emissions of Railway Transportation*

China's rail transport also made progress in promoting energy utilization efficiency and decreasing carbon dioxide emissions. In 2009, the comprehensive energy consumption per unit of transportation mileage for railways was further decreased. For example, the energy consumption of national railway[4] transport enterprises amounted to

---

[4] "National railway" herein only includes state-owned railway and does not include state-controlled joint-venture railways. Such transportation infrastructures as railways

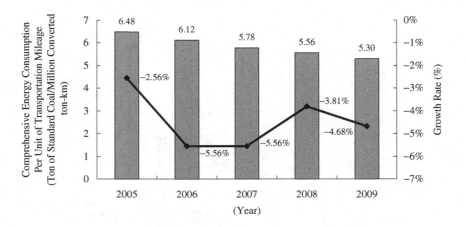

Figure 3.3   Annual Change in Comprehensive Energy Consumption Per Unit of Railway Transportation Mileage
Source: Compiled from the *Railway Statistical Bulletin* (2009), published by the Ministry of Railways of China.

15,975.5 ktons of coal, a reduction by 963.6 ktons or 5.7% compared with that in 2008. From 2005 to 2009, railway comprehensive energy consumption per unit of transportation mileage in China maintained a steady decline; the energy consumption for 2009 was 5.3 tons of standard coal/million converted ton-km, as shown in Figure 3.3.

Furthermore, railway emission of main pollutants was reduced. Chemical oxygen demand and emission by national railway transportation enterprises was 2,214.39 tons in 2009, decreasing by 91.07 tons and 4.0% down compared with that in 2008; emission of SO_2 was

---

and highways were only invested in and operated by the state before China implemented a market-based economy; after China implemented its market-based economy, the Central Government and local governments constructed joint-venture railways in the early 1980s. Beginning in the new millennium, the Government encouraged social funds to engage in the construction of railways in various forms such as bond financing, project financing and equity financing. The Government combined government investment and social investment at home and abroad and protected legitimate rights and interests in risk and profit. By the end of 2007, joint-venture railways reached 31 lines with 9,516.6 km of business mileage, which signifies that multiplex investment patterns were primarily adopted in the construction of railways.

Table 3.3   Emission of Main Pollutants in National Railways

Item	Unit	2006	2007	2008	2009
Emission of SO_2	1000 tons	46.2	43.6	42.3	40.2
Chemical oxygen demand and emission	tons	2,590.14	2,453.93	2,305.46	2,214.39

Source: Compiled from the *2009 Railway Statistical Bulletin*, published by the Ministry of Railways of China.

40.2 ktons, decreasing by 2.1 ktons and 5.0% down compared with that in 2008, as shown in Table 3.3. Meanwhile, China's railway transportation enterprises actively developed greenery along railway lines; as a result, greened mileage reached 35,300 km, increasing by 2,200 km and 6.7% up compared with that in 2008.

3.2 Airports and Cargo Hubs

3.2.1 *Airports, Aviation Cities and Aviation Mileage*

In 2009, investment in the infrastructure of civil aviation increased greatly in China. Fixed asset investment by the entire civil aviation industry was 60 billion RMB; the number of domestic civil airports (certified) increased from 160 in 2008 to 166 in 2009. Among them, 165 airports and 163 cities had scheduled flights, and the area of newly added terminal buildings in civil airports totaled 660,000 m^2.[5] Figure 3.4 shows the total mileage of civil aviation airlines and the total mileage of international airlines in 2004–2008. China newly added six cities with scheduled flights in 2009, further enlarging the domestic airline coverage and increasing the total aviation mileage.

---

[5] 2009 Statistical Bulletin of Nationwide Airports, Civil Aviation Administration of China, 2010.

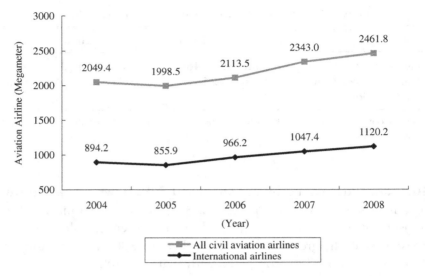

Figure 3.4   Total Mileage of Civil Aviation Airlines and International Airlines for 2004–2008

Source: Data from the *China Statistical Yearbook* (2004–2008), published by the National Bureau of Statistics of China.

3.2.2 *Transportation Volume and Safety*

In spite of the impact of the international financial crisis, all indicators of airport transportation still grew in 2009, as seen in Table 3.4.

In 2009, freight throughput reached 9.46 million tons, 7.13% up compared with that in 2008. Among that, freight throughput of domestic flights reached 6.25 million tons, 10.85% up compared with that in 2008 (including 0.5 million tons of freight throughput to Hong Kong, Macao and Taiwan, 2.45% up compared with that in 2008), and that of international flights reached 3.21 million tons, 0.32% up compared with that in 2008.

By the end of October 2009, China's safety record of civil aviation reached 59 months and more than 17.4 million hours. The Civil Aviation Administration of China was given the Outstanding

Table 3.4   Operations of China's Civil Aviation for 2005–2009

Item	Unit	2005	2006	2007	2008	2009
Passenger transportation	Millions	138.27	159.68	185.76	192.51	—
Passenger throughput	Million person-trips	—	331.97	287.59	405.76	486.06
Freight transportation	1,000 tons	3,067	3,494	4,018	4,076	4,455
Freight throughput	Million tons	—	7.53	8.61	8.83	9.46
Number of take-offs/landings	Million times	—	3.49	3.94	4.23	4.84

Source: Compiled from the *China Statistical Yearbook* (2009), *Statistics Bulletin of Civil Airports* (2006–2009) and *2009 National Statistics Bulletin*, published by the National Bureau of Statistics of China.

Contribution Award by the Flight Safety Foundation[6] on November 3. In the past decade, China's civil aviation transportation major accident rate was 0.21/million hours, lower than the global average of 0.29/million hours, which means that China's flight transportation safety has attained advanced international standards.[7]

3.2.3 *Aviation Freight Centers*

In 2009, under keen international competition in aviation logistics, aviation freight companies at home and abroad continued to speed up the integration of the aviation market in China and successively established aviation transshipment centers. In February 2009, Federal

---

[6] The international Flight Safety Foundation, a non-profit non-governmental foundation, is one of the most influential professional international foundations in the field of flight safety. The Outstanding Contribution Award was set up in 1949 by the Foundation, with the purpose of awarding organizations or individuals worldwide that made significant contributions in promoting flight safety.

[7] "The Civil Aviation Administration of China was awarded the 'Outstanding Contribution Award' due to 59 months of safe flights", www.gov.cn, November 3, 2009. http://www.gov.cn/jrzg/2009-11/03/content_1455612.htm.

Express officially launched its Asia-Pacific transshipment hub in Guangzhou. It currently operates 124 take-offs each week at Guangzhou Airport, with flights mainly connecting Southeast Asia and handling cross-border transportation. In June 2009, Shunfeng Express Delivery's transshipment hub began construction at Hangzhou Xiaoshan International Airport, with a total building area of 9,289 m^2 costing 19 million RMB. In January 2010, Hangzhou Xiaoshan International Airport Co., Ltd. and Shunfeng Express Delivery (China) Company officially signed an agreement to invest 1 billion HKD in the project of Shunfeng's airmail express transportation hub in China, which is expected to be finished in 2014. By then flights from Hangzhou Airport will cover the nation's 17 economically most prosperous large and medium-sized cities as well as Hong Kong, Taiwan, Japan and South Korea, with 52 take-offs each day, a daily throughput of 1,076 tons and an annual throughput of about 270,000 tons.

3.2.4 *Direct Flights between the Mainland and Taiwan*

In December 2008, the first two-way direct flight was opened in the North Corridor between Mainland China and Taiwan; in July 2009, the second two-way direct flight in the North Corridor and the first one in the South Corridor were officially launched. Therefore, the number of two-way direct-flight corridors increased to three, providing the necessary conditions for implementation of scheduled flights between the Mainland and Taiwan.

The Cross-Strait Air Transportation Supplement Protocol indicates that cross-strait services will be opened with scheduled passenger and cargo transport services, among which will be 28 round-trip flights for scheduled freight flights and chartered flights. As one of two newly opened two-way direct-flight routes, the second two-way direct-flight corridor in the north can effectively relieve the burden of flights between Beijing, Shandong, the northeast region and Taiwan, relieving air traffic, shortening the flight distance and serving as a good supplement for the first cross-strait North Corridor. The two-way cross-strait direct flight in the South Corridor shortens the distance between the south central region, the southwest region and Taiwan without detouring through Hong Kong and shortens the one-way distance of flights from Guangzhou and Xiamen to Taiwan by about 20 km and 150 km, respectively.[8]

3.3 Seaports and Inland Waterways

3.3.1 *Scale of Investment*

From 2005 to 2009, China maintained a steady increase in the scale of investment in water transportation construction, as seen in Table 3.5. In 2009, the construction of waterways kept increasing — China invested 105.988 billion RMB in the construction of coastal and inland waterways, 7.3% up compared with that in 2008; construction investment in coastal waterways and inland waterways were respectively 75.832 billion RMB and 30.157 billion RMB. In 2009, the key investment in China's water transportation was in inland waterways, with total investment increasing by 55.6% compared with that in 2008.

The investment in water transportation is mainly in the construction and renovation of ports and expansion of berths. In 2009, China constructed and renovated (expanded) 158 berths in coastal ports,

Table 3.5   Investment in Water Transportation Infrastructure in China for 2005–2009 (Unit: Billion RMB)

Item	2005	2006	2007	2008	2009
Investment in coastal and inland waterways	68.877	86.918	88.648	98.734	105.988
Investment in coastal waterways	57.624	70.797	72.011	79.349	75.832
Investment in inland waterways	11.253	16.121	16.637	19.385	30.157

Source: Compiled from the *2009 Statistical Bulletin of Highway and Waterway Transportation Industry*, published by the Ministry of Transport of China.

---

[8] "Cross-strait opened two 2-way direct-flight routes on South and North", Xinhua Net, July 29, 2009.

increasing the throughput capacity by 338.58 million tons; among them, 85 berths were of the 10,000-ton class, with an increased throughput capacity of 319.21 million tons. China constructed and renovated (expanded) 312 berths in inland ports, increasing the throughput capacity by 104.72 million tons; among them, 17 berths were of the 10,000-ton class, with an increased throughput capacity of 31.95 million tons.[9]

3.3.2 Scale of Navigation Routes, Ports and Vessels

Along with the gradual increase in the scale of investment in water transportation construction, the scale of infrastructure of China's water transportation has grown and the transportation structure has been aligned and optimized. For annual changes between 2005 and 2009, the number of ports with throughput in the 10,000-ton class in China increased rapidly at an average of 130 per year. Although the number of vessels for water transportation decreased year by year, their net payload increased year by year, and the number of large-scale vessels with higher payload increased, which reflected an effective adjustment in water transportation structure. The mileage of inland water channels and graded water channels remains stable (Table 3.6).

3.3.3 Scale of Transportation and Safety

In 2009, total freight traffic and freight flows of waterways in China both increased compared with that in 2008; the pace of growth of total freight traffic in 2008 and 2009 was 4.7% and 8.3%, measuring only 1/3 and 2/3 of the growth rates in 2007 respectively. Freight flows in 2008 decreased 21.8% compared with that in 2007. Although freight flows in 2009 increased, it was still lower than that in 2007, which shows that waterway transportation of cargo in China was greatly affected by the international financial crisis. Details are given in Table 3.7.

---

[9] *2009 Statistical Bulletin of Highway and Waterway Transportation Industry*, published by the Ministry of Transportation of China, 2010.

Table 3.6 Scale of Infrastructure of Water Transportation of China for 2005–2009

Item	Unit	2005	2006	2007	2008	2009
Berths in national ports for production	Pieces	35,242	35,453	35,947	31,050*	31,429*
Berths in coastal ports	Pieces	4,298	4,511	4,701	5,119*	5,320*
Berths in inland ports	Pieces	30,944	30,942	31,246	25,931*	26,109*
Berths with 10,000 tons of throughput	Pieces	1,034	1,203	1,337	1,416	1,554
Vessels for water transportation	1,000 pieces	207.3	194.4	191.8	184.2	176.9
Net payload of vessels for water transportation	Million tons	101.8	110.3	118.8	124.2	146.1
Navigation mileage of inland water channels	1,000 km	123.3	123.4	123.5	122.8	123.7
Graded channels	1,000 km	61.0	61.0	61.2	61.1	61.5

Note: Statistics of berths in national ports for production marked with "*" are based on the third data census on national ports conducted on June 30, 2008, with some adjustment in the scope of statistics compared with that in 2007.

Source: Compiled from the *Statistical Bulletin of Highway and Waterway Transportation Industry* (2005–2009), published by the Ministry of Transport of China.

Table 3.7 Operations of Waterway Transportation in China for 2005–2009

Item	Unit	2005	2006	2007	2008	2009
Passenger transportation	Millions	202.27	220.47	228.35	203.34	223
Passenger flows	Billion person-km	6.78	7.36	7.78	5.92	6.94
Freight traffic	Million tons	2,196.48	2,487.03	2,811.99	2,945.10	3,190
Freight flows	Billion ton-km	4,967.23	5,548.58	6,428.49	5,026.27	5,755.67
Container transportation	Million TEUs	19.40	23.30	29.53	—	30.11

Source: Compiled from the *China Statistical Yearbook* (2009), published by the National Bureau of Statistics of China; the *2009 National Statistics Bulletin*; and related data from the *2009 Statistical Bulletin of Highway and Waterway Transportation Industry*, published by the Ministry of Transport of China.

In 2009, the waterway safety conditions of China remained stable with improved water rescue capability. In 2009, the number of accidents for waterway vessels was 358, 4.7% up compared with that in 2008; yet the number of deaths was 336, 4.3% lower than that in 2008. The number of sunken ships was 199, 6.6% down compared with that in 2008; the direct economic loss induced was 347 million RMB, 33.1% down compared with that in 2008. Within the realm of China's rescue responsibility, 19,128 Chinese and foreign persons were in danger, among whom 18,397 were rescued to safety, yielding a rescue success rate of 96.2%. The number of vessels in danger was 2,090; among those 1,588 were rescued successfully, resulting in a success rate of 76.0%.

3.3.4 *Conditions of Large-Scale Ports*

The number of ports with a cargo throughput of more than 100 million tons increased from 16 in 2008 to 20 in 2009, including 16 coastal ports and four inland ports, as seen in Table 3.8. In 2009, there were 16 ports in China with a container throughput of over 1 million TEUs. Table 3.9 shows the specific container throughput.

3.4 Highways

3.4.1 *Scale of Investment*

China continually increased its investment in highways from 2005 to 2009, during which the growth rate of investment in 2007–2008 dropped to 4–6%. In 2009, the Government greatly increased the scale of investment in highways, putting 966.88 billion RMB in the construction of highways, which was a 40.52% increase compared with that in 2008. Figure 3.5 shows the details.

In terms of investment in various provinces, there were nine provinces with an annual highway investment of over 40 billion RMB, i.e., Hunan (66.85 billion), Guangdong (58.93 billion), Shanxi (56.31 billion), Sichuan (53.90 billion), Zhejiang (49.26 billion), Hebei (48.93 billion), Shaanxi (48.93 billion), Fujian (45.48 billion) and Hubei (41.23 billion).

Table 3.8   Ports of China with Cargo Throughput over 100 Million Tons, 2009

Port	Cargo Throughput (100 Million Tons)	Coastal Port?	Port	Cargo Throughput (100 Million Tons)	Coastal Port?
Ningbo-Zhoushan Port	5.77	Y	Shanghai Port	4.95	Y
Tianjin Port	3.81	Y	Guangzhou Port	3.64	Y
Qingdao Port	3.15	Y	Dalian Port	2.72	Y
Qinhuangdao Port	2.49	Y	Suzhou Port	2.46	Y
Shenzhen Port	1.94	Y	Rizhao Port	1.81	Y
Yingkou Port	1.76	Y	Tangshan Port	1.76	Y
Huzhou Port	1.49	N	Nantong Port	1.36	N
Yantai Port	1.24	Y	Zhanjiang Port	1.18	Y
Nanjing Port	1.21	N	Xiamen Port	1.11	Y
Lianyungang Port	1.08	Y	Jiangyin Port	1.01	N

Source: Data from the *2009 Statistical Bulletin of Highway and Waterway Transportation Industry*, published by the Ministry of Transport of China.

3.4.2 *Highway Mileage and Development of Highway Network*

The highway mileage in China has continued to increase and the scale of its highway network expands year by year. By the end of 2009, the total highway mileage reached 3,860,800 km, increasing by 130,700 km compared with that in 2008; the mileage of graded highways reached 3,056,300 km, which accounted for 79.2% of the total highway mileage, increasing by 277,700 km compared with that in 2008; the mileage of highways graded G-2 and above reached

Table 3.9   Ports of China with Container Throughput over 1 Million TEUs in 2009

Port	Container Throughput (Million TEUs)	Port	Container Throughput (Million TEUs)
Shanghai Port	25.00	Shenzhen Port	18.25
Guangzhou Port	11.19	Ningbo-Zhoushan Port	10.50
Qingdao Port	10.26	Tianjin Port	8.70
Xiamen Port	4.68	Dalian Port	4.57
Lianyungang Port	3.03	Foshan Port	2.92
Suzhou Port	2.72	Yingkou Port	2.54
Yantai Port	1.40	Quanzhou Port	1.25
Fuzhou Port	1.22	Nanjing Port	1.21

Source: Data from the *2009 Statistical Bulletin of Highway and Waterway Transportation Industry*, published by the Ministry of Transport of China.

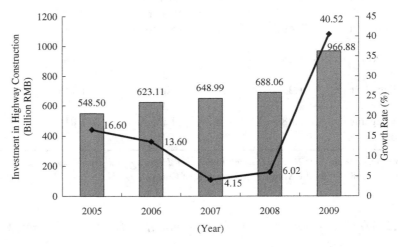

Figure 3.5   Scale of China's Highway Investment and Growth Rate for 2005–2009

Source: Data from the *2009 Statistical Bulletin of Highway and Waterway Transportation Industry*, published by the Ministry of Transport of China.

425,200 km which accounted for 11% of the total highway mileage, 0.3% up compared with that in 2008; the mileage of G-3 highways, G-4 highways and sub-standard highways totaled 37,900 km, 2,252,000 km and 804,600 km, respectively.

Regarding the construction of expressways in China, as of 2009, the total traffic mileage of expressways reached 65,000 km, ranking No. 2[10] in the world. The traffic mileage of newly added expressways in one year in Hubei, Chongqing, Gansu, Shaanxi and Anhui all exceeded 300 km. Seven provinces (Henan, Shandong, Guangdong, Jiangsu, Hebei, Zhejiang and Hubei) had an expressway mileage exceeding 3,000 km.

Meanwhile, China continued to increase the density of highway construction, paving highways through 95% of rural regions and towns. From 2005 to 2009, the density of China's highways increased from 20.1 km/100 km^2 to 40.22 km/100 km^2, with a total growth rate of more than 100% in five years. By the end of 2009, 99.6% of villages and towns in China had paved highways, which increased 0.36% compared with that at the end of 2008; 95.77% of all administrative villages in China had paved highways, which was an increase of 2.91% compared with that at the end of 2008. In April 2009, China officially began to rebuild the highway between Bomi Zamu of Tibet and Motuo County (Motuo Highway), meaning that the road to the last county without highways will soon be in place.

3.4.3 Scale of Transportation Volume

In 2009, the highway freight volume of commercial vehicles in China reached 21.28 billion tons, 11.01% up compared with that in 2008; the growth rate of freight volume in 2009 was basically restored to the level before the international financial crisis (i.e., a 9.24% growth rate in 2006 and an 11.8% growth rate in 2007). Freight flows in 2009 reached 3,718.88 billion ton-km, increasing by 13.15% compared with that in 2008, and the growth rate was restored to the average level in 2006–2007 before the international financial crisis. The average transportation distance of freight maintained its upward trend, marking the increase in proportion of cross-regional and long-distance transportation in China. Table 3.10 shows the details.

---

[10] He Liming, "The development of our country's logistics industries in 2009, and the outlook in 2010", The 2010 China Logistics Development Seminar and the Awards Assembly of A-level Logistics Enterprises, China, 2010.

Table 3.10   Operations of China Highway for 2005–2009

Item	Unit	2005	2006	2007	2008	2009
Passenger transportation of commercial vehicles	Billions	16.97	18.61	20.51	26.82	27.79
Passenger flows	Billion person-km	929.21	1,013.09	1,150.68	1,247.61	1,351.14
Freight volume of commercial vehicles	Billion tons	13.42	14.66	16.39	19.17*	21.28*
Freight flows	Billion ton-km	869.32	975.43	1,135.47	3,286.82*	3,718.88*
Average transportation distance of freight	km	64.79	66.50	69.30	171.48*	174.77*

Note: Data marked with "*" were re-defined with commercial vehicles within the statistical scope; these are commercial vehicles registered with the Highway Transportation Management Department. The scope of statistical data in 2008 and 2009 was adjusted, compared with that in 2007.

Source: Compiled from the *China Statistical Yearbook* (2009) and the *2009 National Statistics Bulletin*, published by the National Bureau of Statistics of China.

3.5 Logistics Parks and Dry Ports

3.5.1 *Scale of Logistics Parks*

In 2009, the logistics parks in China continued to grow in number, including 200 newly added logistics parks that are under planning, construction or have been completed, with a total area of 431.34 million m². Meanwhile, data gathered by the China Federation of Logistics and Purchasing on ten capital cities and three municipalities showed that there were 132 logistics parks in these 13 cities with a total area of 113.4 km².[11]

In terms of nationwide logistics parks infrastructure in 2009, completed logistics parks in operation accounted for 44.1%,

---

[11] Jiang Chaofeng, "Review of storage industry for 2009 and its prospect for 2010", The 2010 China Logistics Development Seminar and the Awards Assembly of A-level Logistics Enterprises, China, 2010.

increasing by 30 compared with that in 2008; those under planning accounted for 27.8%, increasing by 30 compared with that in 2008; while logistics parks under construction accounted for 28.1%.

3.5.2 Construction of Dry Ports

In October 2002, China officially opened its first dry port, Chaoyang Port, and by 2010 there were 35 dry ports in China, of which the main ones are shown in Table 3.11. Dry ports need to collaborate

Table 3.11 Development Status of Main Dry Ports in China

Location of Dry Ports	Area (1,000 m²)	Location of Home Ports	Transportation Medium	Note
Zhengzhou	3,140	Tianjin	Highway	
Shijiazhuang	210	Tianjin	Highway	
Ganzhou	2,000	Xiamen	Railway	Under construction
Xi'an	7,680	Tianjin, Qingdao, Lianyungang	Railway	Under construction
Baotou	28	Tianjin	Highway	
Linyi	100	Rizhao	Highway	
Sanming	—	Xiamen	Railway	Under construction
Houma	160	Lianyungang	Railway	
Jinhua	25	Ningbo	Highway	
Yiwu	300	Ningbo	Highway	
Shaoxing	—	Ningbo	—	
Yuyao	80	Ningbo	Highway	
Quzhou	260	Ningbo	Highway	
Shenyang	500	Yingkou	Highway	
Nanchang	—	Xiamen	Railway	Under construction
Harbin	350	Dalian, Yingkou, Jinzhou	Railway	
Changchun	200	Dalian	Railway	
Kunming	5	Guangzhou	Railway	
Yinchuan	120	Lianyungang	Railway	
Huinong	226	Tianjin	Railway	
Pinggu	600	Tianjin	Highway	
Yingtan	130	Ningbo	Highway	

with coastal home ports to operate. China's home ports mainly include ports in Tianjin, Qingdao, Dalian, Guangzhou, Ningbo, Lianyungang, Xiamen, Rizhao, Yingkou and Jinzhou.

The construction of dry ports in China reflects the mutual need of coastal ports and inland cities for regional trade development, and realizes the win-win cooperation of both parties. First, coastal ports actively cooperate with inland regions to construct dry ports in order to attract freight sources and enlarge the ports' scope of coverage. For example, coastal Tianjin Port constructed inland dry ports in northern cities with logistics centers and border ports to set up transport channels connecting the inland and coastal ports. Second, inland regions actively seek the construction of dry ports in order to develop the local economy and trade. For example, the inland city of Nanchang joined coastal Xiamen Port, Shenzhen Port and Ningbo Port to construct a dry port through sea-rail inter-modal transportation, linking local import and export trading with coastal international freight lines; inland Harbin, Changchun and Shenyang cooperated with coastal Dalian Port to construct dry ports to expand the scope of freight sources for the Dalian region, as well as to speed up the trading between the inland cities and the world.

3.6 Communication and Information Infrastructure

3.6.1 *Scale of Communication Infrastructure*

By the end of 2009, China had 313.69 million fixed telephone stations, among which urban stations accounted for 211.78 million and rural stations accounted for 101.91 million. China had 747.38 million units of mobile telephones at the end of 2009, increasing by 106.14 million compared with that in 2008. The total number of fixed telephones and mobile telephones in 2009 reached 1,061.07 million units; telephone ownership rate reached 79.9 sets/100 persons. The number of people in China surfing the Internet in 2009 reached 380 million, with 350 million people on broadband Internet, and the rate of Internet usage reached 28.9% of the entire population.

The total revenue of China's postal and telecommunication services in 2009 was 2.73 trillion RMB, 14.6% up compared with that in 2008. The total value of its postal service in 2009 reached 163.2 billion RMB, 16.4% up compared with that in 2008, and the total value of its telecommunication service reached 2.57 trillion RMB, 14.4% up compared with that in 2008.

3.6.2 Construction of Logistics Information Platform

Hosted by governments at all levels, China accelerated the construction of a public logistics information platform in 2009.[12] Eleven provinces, districts and cities such as Zhejiang, Shandong and Shanghai jointly signed the *Provincial Public Information Platform Construction Agreement* in July 2007, to promote sharing of logistics information among different cities. Under the leadership of the Central Government, related government departments of 16 provinces, districts and cities, and more than 30 enterprises began to promote piloting the unified logistics software through various forms of cooperation.[13] In addition, the governing departments of the Pearl River Delta and Chongqing city began experimenting with the construction of an information-based test area in their jurisdiction.

Besides the construction of a logistics information platform promoted by governments at all levels, China Mobile, China Unicom and China Telecom, as the three largest telecommunication enterprises in China, leveraged their advantages of telecommunication infrastructure and mobile networks to put forward information-based logistics solutions for enterprises. These include "Logistics New Space" by China Unicom, "Mobile Logistics" by China Mobile and "One-Stop Logistics Information Service Platform" by China Telecom.

---

[12] Logistics information platforms generally refer to information service systems including logistics information networks for publishing, delivering and sharing public information, software and so on.

[13] "Eleven provinces and cities in China signed an agreement to construct a public logistics information platform", Financial News Network, July 10, 2009. http://content.caixun.com/NE/01/f5/NE01f5q2.shtm.

3.6.3 *Development and Technological Application of Logistics Information*

In 2009, the total value of China's radio frequency identification (RFID) market reached 8.51 billion RMB, 29.3% up compared with that in 2008. The Government spearheaded the application of RFID technology through various measures. RFID is touted as an impressive technology in the market, and considered an industry prominently supported by the Government.

In 2009, R&D and the application of the Internet of Things (IOT) were further promoted, especially in fields like medicine management, traffic management, agriculture and logistics. In September 2009, the Transducer Network Standard Workgroup was established, after which the State Council approved the construction of the National Transducer Innovation Demonstration Zone (National Transducer Information Center) in Wuxi city; in November 2009, the Wuxi IOT/Transducer Research Center was officially established to build up the technological R&D of IOT and a public platform for application services. In December 2009, the IOT Engineering Research Center was officially established at Dalian Maritime University, which marked the overall commencement of the development of the Internet of Things in Dalian city.

CHAPTER 4

China's Logistics Development by Region

Logistics, being an economic phenomenon, reflects the state of a nation's economic activities and regional characteristics. This chapter takes a closer look at China's logistics development by region. Detailed data and the economic features of three major geographical regions are examined to provide an in-depth understanding of the regions' logistics status, in terms of history, geography, location and transportation infrastructure. Logistics enterprises, foreign trade and government policies, as well as port facilities are also discussed.

The chapter then focuses on an analysis of logistics development in several of the most concentrated and well-endowed logistics clusters — the Yangtze River Delta, the Pearl River Delta and the Bohai Rim Region, as well as Hong Kong, Macao and Taiwan. Together, these clusters and areas form the backbone of China's flourishing economy and blossoming logistics industry. The impact of the international financial crisis and foreign competition on the logistics enterprises is also addressed.

4.1 Regional Difference in the Development of China's Logistics

4.1.1 *Partition of China's Economic Regions*

China exhibits typical signs of imbalanced economic development due to various factors including its massive territory, historical evolution and geographical location. According to the extent of economic development and geographical location, Mainland China can be divided into three economic regions as depicted in Figure 4.1. The Eastern economic zone consists of 11 provinces (municipalities) including Beijing, Tianjin, Hebei, Liaoning, Shanghai, Jiangsu, Zhejiang, Fujian, Shandong, Guangdong and Hainan; the Central economic zone consists of eight provinces (municipalities) including Shanxi, Jilin, Heilongjiang, Anhui, Jiangxi, Henan, Hubei and Hunan; the Western economic zone consists of 12 provinces including Guangxi, Inner Mongolia, Sichuan,

Figure 4.1   Partition of China's Economic Regions: Eastern, Central and Western

Chongqing, Guizhou, Yunnan, Tibet, Shaanxi, Gansu, Ningxia, Qinghai and Xinjiang.

4.1.2 *Analysis of the Differences in China's Regional Economic Development*

The Eastern region is 1,069,400 km^2 in size, accounting for 11.13% of the total area; its population is 528 million, accounting for 40% of the total population, as shown in Figures 4.2 and 4.3. Having the coastal advantage, the Eastern region has the highest level of opening-up and the most advanced economy. The regional GDP and added values of the primary industry, the secondary industry and the

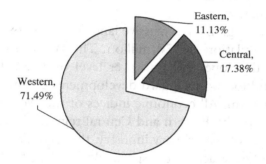

Figure 4.2   Size of Area of Three Main Regions in China

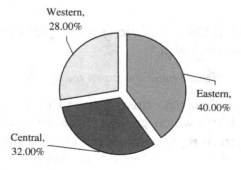

Figure 4.3   Size of Population of Three Main Regions in China

tertiary industry account respectively for 57.9%, 40.0%, 53.2% and 56.4% of the national values; and the total value of imports and exports accounts for more than 90% of the national amount. See Table 4.1 for details.

The Central region has an area of 1,669,800 km², accounting for 17.38% of the total area; its population is 422 million, accounting for 32% of the total population. As the hub connecting the Eastern and Western regions, the Central region is an important transportation hub and cargo distribution center of China, with the level of economic development falling between that of the Eastern and Western regions. Its regional GDP and added values of the primary industry, the secondary industry and the tertiary industry account respectively for 23.6%, 34.1%, 26.8% and 23.8% of the national values, and the total import and export value is less than 5% of that of the nation.

The Western region has a massive land area of 6,869,300 km² and the smallest population at 370 million. The Western region is economically less developed with a lower level of external orientation, due to its inland location, laggard development, elevated topography and complex terrain. All economic indices of the Western region are lower than that of the Eastern and Central regions: its regional GDP and added values of the primary industry, the secondary industry and the tertiary industry account respectively for 18.5%, 25.9%, 20.0% and 19.8% of the national total, and the total value of imports and exports measures a mere 4.1% of the national figure.

4.1.3 *Development Characteristics of the Logistics Industry in the Eastern Region*

Impact of the international financial crisis on the logistics market

The international financial crisis spread all over the world in the second half of 2008, which greatly affected China's imports and exports. The Eastern region was visibly affected due to its export-based economy; the region's logistics market exhibited an obvious sign of slowdown. From January to November 2009, for Shanghai

Table 4.1 Main Economic Indices of the Three Regions in 2009 (Unit: Billion RMB)

Region	Regional GDP		Added Value of Primary Industry		Added Value of the Secondary Industry		Added Value of Tertiary Industry		Total Value of Imports and Exports	
	Total Value	Proportion	Total Value	Proportion	Total Value	Proportion	Total Value	Proportion	Total Value	Proportion
Eastern region	20,973.6	57.9%	1,423.8	40.0%	8,504.0	53.2%	7,338.2	56.4%	2,013.8	91.1%
Central region	8,562.8	23.6%	1,213.0	34.1%	4,278.7	26.8%	3,098.1	23.8%	105.6	4.8%
Western region	6,686.8	18.5%	919.8	25.9%	3,186.1	20.0%	2,580.8	19.8%	91.5	4.1%

Note: "Proportion" means the percentage of the regional value out of the national total.
Source: Data from the *Economic and Social Development Statistics Bulletin* of 31 provinces.[1]

---

[1] The 31 provinces in this document refers to administrative units of provinces, municipalities and autonomous regions.

Port, cargo throughput was 534.42 million tons, 1% down compared with that in 2008; cargo throughput of foreign trade was 232.76 million tons, 8.7% down compared with that in 2008; container throughput was 22.6 million TEUs, 12.3% down compared with that in 2008.

Total value of logistics demand in the Eastern region

The GDP of the Eastern region in 2009 was 20.97 trillion RMB, accounting for 57.9% of the national GDP, and was much higher than that of the Central and Western regions. The economy of such an advanced region could definitely generate a considerable amount of demand for logistics. Hence, the total value of logistics demand in the Eastern region was far above that in the Central and Western regions, as can be seen from several indicators in Table 4.2.

First, the total freight traffic and freight flows in the Eastern region were obviously higher than that in the Central and Western regions. The total freight traffic in the Eastern region in 2008 was 11.6 billion tons, accounting for 44.8% of that in the nation; whereas the values for the Central region and the Western region respectively accounted for 30.9% and 24.3% of that in the nation. Freight flows in the Eastern region in 2008 was 7,031.7 billion ton-km, accounting for 63.8% of that in the nation, whereas the values for the Central region and the Western region accounted respectively for 21.4% and 14.8% of that in the nation (as shown in Table 4.2).

Second, cargo throughput of the Eastern ports was the highest among all national ports. In 2009, cargo throughput of the main coastal ports of the Eastern region was 6.5 billion tons, accounting for 94.1% of the national volume; in terms of geographical position, the top ten container ports of China are located in the Eastern region. Container throughput in 2009 was 98.7 million TEUs, accounting for 81.7% of the national volume.

Third, the air transportation industry is well-developed. Airport cargo throughput of the Eastern region in 2009 was 7.7 million tons, accounting for 81.3% of the national volume, as shown in

Table 4.2   Total Freight Traffic, Freight Flows and Proportion of Three Regions in 2008

Region	Freight Traffic		Freight Flows		Port Throughput		Cargo Throughput of Airport	
	Total Volume (Billion Tons)	Proportion (%)	Freight Flows (Billion Ton-km)	Proportion (%)	Total Volume (Billion Tons)	Rate (%)	Total Volume (Million Tons)	Rate (%)
Eastern region	11.6	44.8	7,031.7	63.8	6.5	94.1	7.7	81.3
Central region	8.0	30.9	2,358.1	21.4	0.26	3.7	0.5	5.3
Western region	6.3	24.3	1,640.3	14.8	0.15	2.2	1.3	13.4
Total	25.9	100.0	11,030.1	100.0	6.91	100.0	9.5	100.0

Source: Compiled from the *China Statistical Yearbook* (2008), published by the National Bureau of Statistics of China.

Table 4.2; airport cargo throughput of the Central and Western regions in 2009 was 1.8 million tons, accounting for 18.7% of the national volume.

Advanced transportation infrastructure

Transportation infrastructrure is relatively well established in the Eastern region, forming a comprehensive and three-dimensional transportation system connected by waterway, railway, highway and aviation.

First, the Eastern region has more than 150 ports, forming the most extensive port groups in China, due to its uniquely endowed coastline. Second, the highways and railways are well-developed. By the end of 2008, the total mileage of railways, highways and expressways in the Eastern region was 21,810 km, 1,050,140 km and 25,560 km, accounting for 27.37%, 28.15% and 42.39% of the national totals, respectively. See Table 4.3 for details. Third, the Eastern region is the region with most extensive airlines and the most advanced aviation industry. In 2009, the region had 50 airports, accounting for 30.12% of the nation's total of 166 airports; total take-offs and landings were 2.73 million, accounting for 67.69% of the national value.

Table 4.3 Conditions of Regional Transportation Infrastructure in 2008

Mode	Railway		Highway		Expressway	
Region	Total Mileage (1,000 km)	Proportion (%)	Total Mileage (1,000 km)	Proportion (%)	Total Mileage (1,000 km)	Proportion (%)
Eastern region	21.81	27.37	1,050.14	28.15	25.56	42.39
Central region	28.34	35.56	1,258.94	33.75	18.28	30.32
Western region	29.54	37.07	1,421.08	38.10	16.46	27.29
Total	79.69	100.0	3,730.16	100.0	60.30	100.00

Source: Compiled from the *China Statistical Yearbook* (2009), published by the National Bureau of Statistics of China.

Considerable scale of demand for international logistics

Foreign trade in the Eastern region was well-developed, with considerable demand for and rapid development of international logistics.

The total value of imports and exports of the Eastern region in 2009 reached 2,013.8 billion USD, accounting for 91.08% of the national total; whereas that of the Central region in 2009 reached 105.6 billion USD, accounting for 4.78% of the national amount, and that for the Western region in 2009 reached 91.5 billion USD, accounting for 4.14% of the national amount (Figure 4.4). In 2009, there were five ports in the Eastern region — Shanghai, Shenzhen, Guangzhou, Ningbo-Zhoushan and Qingdao — with an annual container throughput exceeding 10 million TEUs, which ranked among the top ten container ports in the world.

The highly-developed import/export trade attracted many multinational logistics enterprises to accelerate their business disposition in China, and to actively seize the logistics market, thus leading to rapidly developed international logistics in China. For example, Federal Express's Asia-Pacific transshipment hub was officially opened at Guangzhou Baiyun International Airport in 2009, with 16 international freight lines and 136 take-offs/landings at the hub each week.

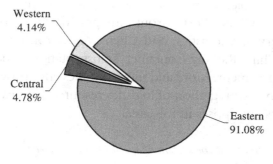

Figure 4.4   Total Value of Imports and Exports for China's Three Regions

Relatively better development of logistics enterprises

First, a pattern of multi form logistics supply entities, constituted by state-owned, foreign-funded and private logistics enterprises, was formed in the Eastern region; the development level of logistics enterprises is obviously higher than that in the Central and Western regions: (1) the Eastern region was the frontline where Maersk, UPS, Exel, TNT, DHL and other world-famous logistics enterprises took the first step into China; (2) COSCO, China Shipping (Group) Company, China Merchants Group and other state-owned logistics enterprises actively and concertedly developed their logistics business; (3) private logistics enterprises swarmed into this region — 25 of the top 30 private logistics enterprises in China entered the Eastern region in 2009.

Second, the logistics enterprises heightened their awareness of strategic cooperation and further strengthened long-term collaboration with client enterprises in the manufacturing industries. In 2009, more and more logistics enterprises in the Eastern region provided clients with integrated logistics services including purchasing, transportation and delivery through signing long-term contracts, setting up strategic alliances and other forms of cooperation with manufacturing enterprises, raw material manufacturers and construction companies.

Third, the trend of scale-based and profession-based development for logistics enterprises became evident, with various forms of accelerated mergers and acquisitions taking place among logistics enterprises, which helped to promote the integrated development of logistics enterprises. For example, mergers and acquisitions were carried out by SINOTRANS; China Post Group integrated its headquarters for express delivery and logistics; and Chengtong Group, China Railway Express and China Railway Container Transportation signed a strategic cooperative agreement. More and more logistics enterprises entered the Eastern region via integration of logistics resources, increasing the density of logistics enterprises in this area.

Gradual improvement of the system of special customs areas

The system of special customs areas was gradually improved, which was helpful for the rapid development of international logistics in this area. By the end of 2009, the Eastern region had built up 41 export processing zones, 19 bonded logistics centers, 11 bonded ports and six comprehensive bonded zones, accounting for 71.93%, 76.00%, 84.62% and 66.67% of the national figures respectively. In addition, all 13 bonded zones and seven bonded logistics parks in China were settled in the Eastern region (Table 4.4).

Rapid development of port logistics

The Eastern region, being the region densest with ports and with the most developed ports, built up four ports groups in the Bohai Rim Region, the Yangtze River Delta, the southeast coast and the Pearl River Delta. In 2009, the throughput of main coastal ports of the Eastern region was 6.5 billion tons, accounting for 94.1% of the national total. Ningbo, Shanghai, Tianjin, Guangzhou, Qingdao, Dalian, Qinhuangdao, Suzhou, Shenzhen and Rizhao Ports were China's top ten ports with the highest throughput. Shanghai, Shenzhen, Guangzhou, Ningbo and Qingdao ranked among the top ten container ports in the world. The foreign trade throughput of Shanghai, Ningbo, Qingdao, Tianjin, Shenzhen and Rizhao Ports was each more than 100 million tons (Table 4.5).

4.1.4 Development Characteristics of the Logistics Industry in the Central and Western Regions

Lagging development of the Central and Western regions

First, the GDP of the Central region and Western region in 2009 was 8,562.8 billion RMB and 6,686.8 billion RMB, accounting for 23.6% and 18.5% of national GDP respectively, far below that of the Eastern region. The economies of the Central and Western regions were relatively underdeveloped, with their total logistics demand lagging behind that of the Eastern region.

Second, the total value of imports and exports of the Central and Western regions in 2009 was 197.1 billion USD, accounting for 8.92% of the national total. Export-based economies of the Central and Western regions were rather slim, which to some extent limited the scale and development of demand for international logistics.

Table 4.4 Development Status of Bonded Logistics Areas (Sites) in China

Type	Locality	Eastern Region (Units)	Nationwide (Units)	Percentage in Eastern Region (%)
Bonded zone	Shanghai Waigaoqiao, Dalian, Tianjin, Qingdao, Zhangjiagang, Ningbo, Fuzhou, Xiamen Xiangyu, Shantou, Guangzhou, Shenzhen, Zhuhai and Haikou	13	13	100.00
Export processing zone	There were a total of 57 export processing zones in China in 2009	41	57	71.93
Bonded logistics center	Nanjing Longtan Port, Suzhou New District, Shanghai Northwest Logistics Park, Tianjin Economic and Technological Development Zone, Dongguan, Zhongshan, Guangzhou Airport, Jiangyin, Taicang, Hangzhou, Qingdao, Rizhao, Xiamen Torch (Xiang'an), Yingkou, Shenyang, Shenzhen Airport, Lianyungang, Nanning and Ningbo Lishe	19	25	76.00
Bonded logistics park	Shanghai Waigaoqiao, Tianjin Port, Qingdao, Zhangjiagang, Ningbo, Xiamen and Shenzhen	7	7	100.00
Bonded port	Shanghai Yangshan, Tianjin East Xinjiang, Dalian Dayao Bay, Hainan Yangpu, Ningbo Mei Shan, Xiamen Haicang, Qingdao Bay, Shenzhen Bay, Guangzhou Nansha, Zhangjiagang and Yantai	11	13	84.62
Comprehensive bonded zone	Suzhou Industrial Park, Tianjin Binhai New Area, Beijing Tianzhu, Haikou, Shanghai Pudong Airport and Kunshan, Jiangsu	6	9	66.67

Source: Compiled from data published by the China Free Trade Export Association. http://www.cfea.org.cn/.

Table 4.5 Development Status of Main Coastal Ports in the Eastern Region in 2009

Rank	Throughput Port Ranking	Million Tons	Container Throughput Port Ranking	Million TEUs	Foreign Trade Throughput* Port Ranking	Million Tons
1	Ningbo-Zhoushan	577	Shanghai	25.00	Shanghai	232
2	Shanghai	495	Shenzhen	18.25	Ningbo-Zhoushan	223
3	Tianjin	381	Guangzhou	11.19	Qingdao	203
4	Guangzhou	364	Ningbo-Zhoushan	10.50	Tianjin	178
5	Qingdao	315	Qingdao	10.26	Shenzhen	130
6	Dalian	272	Tianjin	8.70	Rizhao	120
7	Qinhuangdao	249	Xiamen	4.68	Tangshan	93
8	Suzhou	246	Dalian	4.55	Dalian	90
9	Shenzhen	194	Lianyungang	3.02	Guangzhou	75
10	Rizhao	181	Yingkou	2.54	Lianyungang	60

Note: Data marked with "*" are for January–November 2009; other data are for the whole of 2009. *Source*: Throughput data are compiled from Xinhua Network and related news networks; container throughput data are drawn from "Ranking of top 45 container ports of the world in 2009", China Port 2010 (May); foreign trade throughput data of ports above designated size[2] come from *Cargo Throughput of Foreign Trade of Coastal Ports above the Designated Size (January–November, 2009)*, published by the Ministry of Transport of China.

Third, the overall development level of logistics enterprises in the Central and Western regions was lower. The majority of logistics enterprises in these regions were traditional storage and transportation enterprises which needed improvement in specialization, scale and internationalization. In addition, the income of the main business of logistics enterprises in the Central and Western regions was lower than that of logistics enterprises in the Eastern region.

---

[2] Ports above the designated size are those sea ports with annual cargo throughput over 1 million tons and inland ports with annual cargo throughput over 2 million tons and ports for international trade, for container load and unload, as specified by the Chinese Ministry of Transport.

Fourth, construction of logistics parks in the Central and Western regions lagged behind that in the Eastern region and exhibited an obvious difference in their development. A survey shows that there are 215 logistics parks in the Central and Western regions, accounting for 45.3% of all logistics parks in China; among which the number of logistics parks in operation was 43, accounting for 35.2% of all operating logistics parks in China.[3] The logistics parks in the Central and Western regions are located mainly in the Central Yellow River Delta Economic Zone, Southwest Economic Zone, Central Yangtze River Delta Economic Zone and other parts of the Central region while only a few are located in the Western region, showing a notable regional difference.

Rapid expansion of special customs custodial areas to the Central and Western regions

Processing trade in the Central and Western regions developed rapidly, which led to a rapid establishment of a matching bonded logistics network, as shown in Table 4.6. During the ten years the Government promoted the Great Westward Development policy, the average annual growth rate of processing trade of imports and exports in the Western region reached 25%, higher than that in the Eastern region. Against this backdrop, China Customs actively promoted the construction of a bonded logistics network in the Western region. So far, the Western region has already constructed ten special customs custodial areas with export processing and 49 various bonded custodial areas, thus effectively fostering the rapid development of its processing trade and bonded logistics.

Notable acceleration of construction of transportation infrastructure

Along with the implementation of the Great Western Development strategy and a set of policies leaning towards the Central and Western regions, construction of transportation infrastructure in these regions accelerated noticeably. In 2008, the total mileage of railways, highways

---

[3] China Federation of Logistics and Purchasing, *The Second National Logistics Park Survey Report*, China Logistics Publishing House, Beijing, China, 2008.

Table 4.6 Development Status of Special Customs Custodial Areas in the Central and Western Regions

Type	Time of First Establishment	Scale (Units)	Regional Distribution
Export processing zone	First four national-level export processing zones in the Central and Western regions, i.e., Wuhan, Chengdu, Hunchun, were established by the State Council in April 2004	16	Jiangxi, Sichuan, Hubei, Chongqing, Anhui, Henan, Guangxi, Jilin, Shaanxi, Inner Mongolia, Yunnan and Xinjiang
Bonded port	Guangxi Qinzhou Bonded Port was established in May 2008	2	Guangxi Qinzhou, Chongqing
Comprehensive bonded zone	Guangxi Pingxiang Comprehensive Bonded Zone was established in December 2008	3	Guangxi Pingxiang, Heilongjiang Suifen River, Chongqing Xiyong
Bonded logistics center	Hubei Wuhan Dongxi Lake Bonded Logistics Center was approved in December 2008	6	Shaanxi Xi'an, Hubei Wuhan, Sichuan Chengdu, Hunan Changsha, Shanxi Houma, Jiangxi Nanchang
Cross-border industrial zone	Construction of China-Kazakhstan Horgos Border Cooperation Zone was approved by the State Council in March 2006	1	Xinjiang

Note: Data cover up to the end of 2009. In addition, according to the regional distribution of China in the Seventh Five-Year Plan, Jilin and Heilongjiang come under to the Central region in this table.

Source: China Free Trade Export Association Website. http://www.cfea.org.cn.

and expressways in the Central and Western regions was 57,880 km, 2,680,000 km and 34,740 km, respectively, with growth rates of 2.21%, 4.59% and 10.69%, respectively. Among these, the growth rate of highway construction was particularly high, 1.77% higher than that in the Eastern region.

Along with the implementation of the 4 trillion RMB economic stimulus plan advanced by the Chinese Central Government in 2009, construction of transportation infrastructure for the Central and Western regions was further sped up — highway, railway, aviation and shipping networks have all been enhanced.

First, rapid development was achieved in the construction of expressways. For example, Hunan Province constructed 14 new expressways in 2009 with a total mileage of 1,221 km; Hubei Province constructed new expressways totaling 563 km, making the total mileage in the province 3,282 km; Anhui Province has newly constructed 300 km of expressways, upping the total mileage in the province to 2,800 km.

Second, rapid development of railway construction was achieved in the Central and Western regions in 2009, with the total operating mileage reaching 33,000 km, 9.2% up compared with that in 2008. Great progress was made in construction projects including special passenger lines, cross-regional corridors and hubs. For example, the Wuhan-Guangzhou Special Passenger Line spanning 1,068.6 km is the longest high-speed railway line in the world, effectively shortening the transport time from the Central and Western regions to the Eastern region. Wuhan North Marshalling Station, Guiyang South Marshalling Station, Wuhan Bullet Train and other hub construction projects were entirely or partially constructed to effectively enhance the transportation efficiency of the railway network of the Central and Western regions, and to help speed up the exchange of resources between the Central/Western regions and the Eastern region.

Rapid entry of logistics enterprises into the Western region

First, along with the implementation of the Great Westward Development strategy, well-known logistics enterprises at home and abroad swarmed into the logistics market in the Western region and at an accelerated pace. For example, by the end of 2009, 43 foreign logistics enterprises including UPS, FedEx, TNT, Maersk and 13 well-known domestic logistics enterprises including Modern China Railway and China Railway Express had already entered Chengdu city. Second, foreign well-known logistics real estate developers began to exploit the market of logistics parks in the Central and Western regions. For example, ProLogis constructed Chongqing and Wuhan Logistics Parks in 2006 and Chengdu Logistics Park in 2008. Besides ProLogis, other large-scale enterprises participated in the construction of logistics parks in the Central and Western regions, which effectively enhanced the internationalization of local logistics. All these ushered in such well-known third-party logistics enterprises in the world as TNT and UPS and attracted Adidas, Samsung, Nokia and other World Top 500 Enterprises to locate themselves in the Central and Western regions.

Imbalanced development of logistics within the region

Owing to the differences in geographical location and the level of economic and societal development, logistics development within the Central and Western regions manifested an obvious imbalance. This phenomenon was reflected in the fact that logistics development in key city clusters was very good, while that in other regions still lagged behind. Chengyu City Cluster, Wanjiang City Belt, Central China City Cluster, Wuhan City Cluster, Changsha-Zhuzhou-Xiangtan City Cluster and North Gulf City Cluster had higher development levels of logistics with well-developed infrastructure within the regions and basically complete transportation networks. For instance, in Wanjiang City Belt, by the end of 2009, there were over 200 third-party logistics enterprises above a certain scale and 1,600 km of expressways, forming a "Four Vertical and Three Horizontal" expressway framework, including six interfaces connecting to the Yangtze River Delta.

Important role of inland waterway shipping

The Central and Western regions are endowed with plentiful river and coastal resources — the total mileage of inland waterways is 71,900 km, accounting for 58.6% of that of national inland waterways. The Yangtze River, Yellow River, Huaihe River, Heilongjiang River, Songliao River and other main rivers sprawl all over the Central and Western regions. Supported by inland waterways, railways and highways, the Central and Western regions have engaged Chongqing, Wuhan, Hefei, Harbin and other logistics nodal cities as the core of regional logistics. Composite river-sea transportation and a service-oriented economy have forged a multi-level inland waterway logistics service system, and become an important basis of logistics development in the Central and Western regions.

4.2 Development Status of Logistics in the Yangtze River Delta

The Yangtze River Delta mainly includes Shanghai city, Jiangsu Province and Zhejiang Province, and is the city cluster with the largest economic scale, highest level of opening-up and most advanced logistics industry in China.

4.2.1 *Economic Development Conditions in the Yangtze River Delta*

Total economic value of the region

The Yangtze River Delta is the city cluster with the highest economic value in China. From 2005 to 2008, its average annual growth rate was 17.0%. In 2009, its GDP was 7,179.4 billion RMB, increasing by 9.6% from that in 2008; the pace of growth slowed down visibly in 2009 due to the impact of the international financial crisis, as shown in Table 4.7.

Conditions of industrial development

The Yangtze River Delta is regarded as the base for essential advanced manufacturing industries in China. For example, Shanghai has established six key manufacturing industries: electronics and information technology, automobiles, petrochemicals and fine chemicals, high-grade

Table 4.7   GDP of the Yangtze River Delta

Year	Value (Billion RMB)				Nominal Growth Rate			
	Jiangsu	Zhejiang	Shanghai	Total	Jiangsu	Zhejiang	Shanghai	Average
2005	1,830.6	1,343.8	916.4	4,090.8	22.0%	15.4%	13.5%	17.8%
2006	2,164.5	1,574.3	1,036.6	4,775.4	18.2%	17.2%	13.1%	16.7%
2007	2,574.1	1,878.0	1,218.9	5,671.0	18.9%	19.3%	17.6%	18.8%
2008	3,031.3	2,148.7	1,369.8	6,549.8	17.8%	14.4%	12.4%	15.5%
2009	3,406.1	2,283.2	1,490.1	7,179.4	12.4%	6.3%	8.8%	9.6%

Source: Compiled from the *China Statistical Yearbook* (2006–2009) and related data from the *2009 Statistical Bulletin of National Economic and Social Development* of Jiangsu Province, Zhejiang Province and Shanghai.

steel, set machinery and biomedicine. In 2009, the total industrial value of these six key industries was 1,534.6 billion RMB, 7.3% up compared with that in 2008 and accounting for 64.3% of the total volume of the industrial enterprises in Shanghai above the designated size.[4]

For Jiangsu Province, manufacturing industries in the areas of transportation equipment, medicine, specialized equipment, electric machinery and equipment, communication equipment, computer and other electronic equipment have grown rapidly, exhibiting a trend of rapid development of advanced manufacturing industries.

For Zhejiang Province, manufacturing industries in the fields of general equipment, electric machinery, electric power, chemical material, communication equipment and textile have developed rapidly in recent years. Meanwhile, high-technology industries have also developed swiftly in Zhejiang Province with an added value in 2009 of 177.1 billion RMB, 6.9% up compared with that in 2008.

The average annual growth rate of the industrial added value of large-scale enterprises in the Yangtze River Delta during 2005–2008 was up to 18.9%. In 2009, the added value of industrial enterprises above the designated size in the Yangtze River Delta was 3,011.1 billion RMB (as seen in Table 4.8), 5.7% up compared with that in

---

[4] Industrial enterprises above the designated size are those with annual revenue from principal business over 5 million RMB.

Table 4.8 Industrial Added Value of Large-Scale Enterprises in the Yangtze River Delta

Year	Absolute Value (Billion RMB)				Nominal Growth Rate			
	Jiangsu	Zhejiang	Shanghai	Total	Jiangsu	Zhejiang	Shanghai	Total
2005	811.9	483.1	399.5	1,694.5	25.9%	17.4%	16.6%	21.1%
2006	1,030.9	599.3	445.6	2,075.8	27.0%	24.1%	11.6%	22.5%
2007	1,292.7	757.1	525.1	2,574.9	25.4%	26.3%	17.8%	24.0%
2008	1,475.9	808.3	565.0	2,849.2	14.2%	6.8%	7.6%	10.7%
2009	1,672.7	823.2	515.2	3,011.1	13.3%	1.8%	−8.8%	5.7%

Source: Compiled from the *China Statistical Yearbook* (2006–2009) and related data from the *Statistical Bulletin of National Economic and Social Development* (2006–2009) of Jiangsu Province, Zhejiang Province and Shanghai.

2008; the growth rate declined obviously in 2009 due to the impact of the international financial crisis.

Status of imports and exports

The Yangtze River Delta is the region with the most prosperous foreign trade in China and its total value of imports and exports accounts for more than 1/3 of the national total. From 2005 to 2008, the Yangtze River Delta saw rapid development in import and export trading with an average annual growth rate of up to 21.1%. Owing to the impact of the international financial crisis, the total value of imports and exports in the Yangtze River Delta in 2009 was 804.3 billion USD (as seen in Table 4.9), a 13.1% decrease from that in 2008. But the total volume of imports and exports in the Yangtze River Delta has shown signs of recovery in terms of quarters. For example, the total value of imports and exports in Jiangsu Province in 2009 was 338.8 billion USD, representing a decrease of 13.6% as compared with that in 2008. However, the sliding growth rates of the first half and the first three quarters of 2009 had narrowed.

Meanwhile, exports of high-tech products from the Yangtze River Delta grew. For example, the total export value of mechanical and electrical products as well as high-tech products from Jiangsu Province in

Table 4.9 Total Value of Imports and Exports in the Yangtze River Delta

	Absolute Value (Billion USD)				Nominal Growth Rate			
Year	Jiangsu	Zhejiang	Shanghai	Total	Jiangsu	Zhejiang	Shanghai	Total
2005	227.9	107.4	186.4	521.7	33.4%	26.0%	16.5%	25.4%
2006	284.0	139.2	227.5	650.6	24.6%	29.6%	22.1%	24.7%
2007	349.7	176.9	283.0	808.5	23.1%	27.1%	24.4%	24.3%
2008	392.3	211.1	322.1	925.5	12.2%	19.4%	13.8%	14.5%
2009	338.8	187.7	277.7	804.3	−13.6%	−11.1%	−13.8%	−13.1%

Source: Compiled from the *China Statistical Yearbook* (2005–2009) and related data from the *2009 Statistical Bulletin of National Economic and Social Development* of Jiangsu Province, Zhejiang Province and Shanghai.

2009 was 138.8 billion USD and 92.8 billion USD, which respectively accounted for 69.6% and 46.6% of total exports, and were 1.8% and 2.9% up compared with that in 2008. The total export value of mechanical and electrical products as well as high-tech products from Shanghai in 2009 was 102.6 billion USD and 63.6 billion USD, which respectively accounted for 72.3% and 44.8% of total exports, and were 2.3% and 2.7% up compared with that in 2008.

4.2.2 Main Characteristics of the Development of Logistics in the Yangtze River Delta

Most developed logistics industry in the nation

As the region with the most advanced logistics industry in China, currently the Yangtze River Delta has gathered and cultivated a great number of professional and comprehensive logistics enterprises equipped with logistics service functions such as transportation, storage, packaging, distribution processing, delivery and information processing. Therefore, the region basically has built up a logistics industry chain with fortified functions and a higher level of service.

State-owned large-scale logistics groups including COSCO, China Shipping Container Lines, SINOTRANS, Zhong Chu Development Stock Co., Ltd. and China International Marine Containers, and international logistics enterprises giants including UPS, Maersk, FedEx, Sagawa Express and TNT have successively entered Shanghai, Nanjing, Hangzhou, Suzhou and Ningbo cities and actively grasped the logistics market of the Yangtze River Delta. More than 400 companies from the Global Top 500 have invested in the Yangtze River Delta and transferred their regional headquarters, R&D centers, purchasing and logistics centers there. These moves have greatly escalated the process of regional economic integration in the Yangtze River Delta and played a role in actively promoting logistics integration in the area.[5]

Ports as the key engine for regional logistics development

As one of the regions with the most extensive and advanced ports in China, the Yangtze River Delta has established a port cluster centered around Shanghai, flanked by Ningbo-Zhoushan Port to the south and Yangkou Port to the north, and extending to many ports up along the Yangtze River. The cargo throughput of ports in the Yangtze River Delta in 2009 was 2,952 million tons (as seen in Table 4.10), accounting for more than 40% of the national amount.

Table 4.10   Cargo Throughput of Ports in the Yangtze River Delta

Year	Cargo Throughput of Port (Million Tons)				Nominal Growth Rate			
	Jiangsu	Zhejiang	Shanghai	Total	Jiangsu	Zhejiang	Shanghai	Total
2005	755	479	443	1,677	19.1%	17.4%	16.9%	18.0%
2006	864	552	537	1,953	14.4%	15.2%	21.2%	16.5%
2007	728	621	561	1,910	−15.7%	12.5%	4.5%	−2.2%
2008	1,150	650	582	2,382	58.0%	4.7%	3.7%	24.7%
2009	1,330	1,030	592	2,952	15.7%	58.5%	1.7%	23.9%

Source: Compiled from the *China Statistical Yearbook* (2005–2009) and related data from the *2009 Statistical Bulletin of National Economic and Social Development* of Jiangsu Province, Zhejiang Province and Shanghai.

---

[5] Hu Yile, "SWOT analysis on logistics integration of the Yangtze River Delta", *China Water Transportation*, 2009(5): 72–78.

Ports have already become the core strategic resources of modern logistics in the Yangtze River Delta.

Progress on the construction of the Shanghai international shipping center

In April 2009, the State Council of the PRC issued the *Notes on Promoting the Construction of Shanghai International Financial Center and International Shipping Center*, which signified that the construction of the Shanghai International Shipping Center had been elevated to the national strategic level. After one year of construction, the Shanghai International Shipping Center has achieved results in various phases.

First, Shanghai further strengthened the modern shipping and dispatching system of Shanghai Port through the construction of multiple transportation infrastructures including highways, shipping facilities, a railway network, an aviation hub and transit waterways. Second, the modern shipping service system has been notably enhanced, which mainly entailed the establishment of a market for crew talents, shipping research institutions, development of maritime arbitration, and regulations for ship transactions. Third, Shanghai actively explored the institution of a comprehensive pilot zone for international shipping development through supporting financial policies, promoting tax rebate bills for departure ports and innovating management mechanisms for special customs areas. Fourth, Shanghai accelerated the development of a financial service for the shipping industry. Finally, Shanghai actively improved and regulated the development of the cruise industry.

As Shanghai is a leading city of the Yangtze River Delta, promoting the construction of its International Shipping Center can enhance its abilities to gather resources and spread the pull of the Yangtze River Delta, resulting in a more developed logistics industry in this region. Construction of the Shanghai International Shipping Center should be connected with the regional division of labor and cooperation among the port cities of the Yangtze River Delta, which can only be realized with the important condition of a shipping service system with a clear and ordered structure.

Structural adjustment of the logistics industry

The logistics industry of the Yangtze River Delta is showing signs of a structural change due to the dual factors of the financial crisis and the adjustment in economic structure.

First, in terms of the scale of logistics, the growth rate has slowed down, even shrunk, in the Yangtze River Delta. Taking Shanghai as an example, the total cargo transportation value of various transportation means in 2009 was 769.7 million tons, an 8.8% drop compared with that in 2008. Although the cargo throughput of Shanghai port was 592 million tons, 1.8% up compared with that in 2008, its container throughput was 25 million TEUs, 10.7% lower than that in 2008.

Second, in terms of logistics enterprises, traditional service enterprises and logistics enterprises with a singular logistics service function are less risk-resilient and more affected by the financial crisis; whereas modern logistics enterprises and logistics enterprises with multi-functional logistics services are affected less. In addition, international logistics enterprises are obviously affected by the slow recovery of the global economy and continual suffering of the international logistics market. Meanwhile, domestic consumption demand is still quite brisk under the Government's policy to invigorate domestic demand, so logistics enterprises involved chiefly in domestic logistics business are affected minimally.

Marked improvement in functions of logistics parks including tax–withholding, transition and industry linkage

The service functions of logistics parks have been obviously improved due to the rapid development of logistics parks in the Yangtze River Delta.

First, the Yangtze River Delta has obtained approval to successively set up multi-form and multi-type special customs custodial zones including the Shanghai Yangshan Bonded Harbor Area, Zhejiang Ningbo Meishan Bonded Harbor Area, Jiangsu Province Zhangjiagang Free Trade Zone, Suzhou Industrial Park Comprehensive Bonded Zone,

Shanghai Airport Comprehensive Bonded Zone and Northwest Comprehensive Bonded Logistics Park, and fully extended the bonded logistics functions of logistics parks involved in sea, land and air. Thus the bonded functions of logistics parks in the Yangtze River Delta are gradually improving.

Second, the transshipping function of logistics parks in the Yangtze River Delta has been obviously enhanced. For example, the cross-national delivery and international purchasing business of Shanghai Waigaoqiao Bonded Logistics Park has made some new breakthroughs; the total volume of domestic and international transshipping cargo reached 35% of the national total. The third airport runway and western cargo transportation area have been constructed in Shanghai Pudong Airport Logistics Park, which attracted UPS Shanghai International Transit Center to locate itself there; Hangzhou Xiaoshan International Airport attracted the project of FedEx China Transit Center. The business of this project grew persistently since its operations began in February 2009 to the end of the year, and its tax receipt grossed over 100 million RMB.

Third, the linkage between logistics parks and the industries shows an obvious development trend. Taking Shanghai as an example, the Logistics Center of China Aviation Industry Group has begun its construction in China Yangshan Bonded Harbor Area in order to explore the interconnecting development of manufacturing, trade and logistics. The Waigaoqiao Logistics Center has basically been constructed to be a base for import and export trade and a logistics operation center for more than ten industries such as automobiles, watches, pharmaceuticals and alcohol.[6]

Rapid integration for regional logistics

The Yangtze River Delta is the region in China where logistics integration has been fastest and seen the best results. In 2007, with the

---

[6] Liu Min, "Shanghai 2009 logistics industry development status and its prospects in 2010", http://www.56products.com/hnew/focus/2010-02-01/content13.html.

establishment of a modern logistics joint conference system and the issuance of *Several Measures for Promoting the Development of Joint and Combined Logistics of the Yangtze River Delta*, logistics cooperation in the Yangtze River Delta entered a substantive stage of development, and interconnected development of logistics regions is gradually emerging.

In August 2008, China's State Council Executive Meeting deliberated and approved the *Views on Further Promoting Reform and Opening-up as well as Economic and Social Development*, so that the plan of integrating the Yangtze River Delta, covering two provinces and one city, was officially elevated to the national strategic level and the pace accelerated.

In 2009, new progress was achieved on the integration of the Yangtze River Delta. For example, the governments of the two provinces and one city of the Delta issued the *Views on Promoting the Development of Highway Cargo (Logistics) Integration of the Yangtze River Delta* in July 2009, stipulating that container trucks from Shanghai, Jiangsu Province and Zhejiang Province would be entitled to equal treatment as the locals. This signifies critical progress on the integration of the Yangtze River Delta. In March 2009, they officially issued the Express Service Development Program in the Yangtze River Delta (2009–2013), which raised integration to become one of the general goals; this will be helpful in enhancing the service level of the express delivery service market in the Yangtze River Delta, strengthening its comprehensive capabilities and advancing the level of the industry.

4.3 Development Status of Logistics in the Pearl River Delta

The Pearl River Delta includes Guangzhou, Shenzhen, Zhuhai, Foshan, Jiangmen, Dongguan, Zhongshan, Huizhou and Zhaoqing cities of Guangdong Province. The Delta encompasses a fan-shaped region centered on Guangzhou and flanked by Hong Kong and Macao at each end; the area is 54,740 km^2 with a population of 47.72 million. Located at the junction of China and the Association of

Southeast Asian Nations Free Trade Area, the Pearl River Delta is the region with the best marketization and most complete market system. It is also the economic zone with the highest degree of export orientation and an important gateway of the opening-up policy. Guangdong Province, with its core in the Pearl River Delta, has continually ranked No. 1 in terms of total economic aggregate among all provinces in China for 20 years. Manufacturing enterprises in the Pearl River Delta spearheaded the entry into global production and manufacturing systems, and has become an important manufacturing base for multinational enterprises, laying a solid foundation for the development of the logistics industry.

4.3.1 *Profile of Economic Development in the Pearl River Delta*

GDP of the region

Though it was affected by the global financial crisis, the pace of economic growth and economic operations in the Pearl River Delta has gradually recovered, due to the implementation of policies to greatly increase the domestic demand and adjust its economic structure. The GDP of the Pearl River Delta in 2009 was 3.21 trillion RMB, 9.4% up compared with that in 2008, accounting for 9.6% of the national total, but the growth rate had slowed down obviously. The GDP per capita was 67,321 RMB, which is about 10,000 USD. The main economic indices of the Pearl River Delta in 2009 are shown in Table 4.11; the change in the total value of imports and exports in the Delta during 2005–2009 can be seen in Figure 4.5.

Industrial structure and development

The industrial structure of the Pearl River Delta has already made the transition from an agriculture-based economy to a processing-and-manufacturing-based economy through gradual optimization and upgrading. Currently, the GDP values of the secondary and tertiary industries in national economy are comparable. The added

Table 4.11　Main Economic Indices of the Pearl River Delta in 2009

Region	GDP of Region (Billion RMB)	Total Amount of Investment in Fixed Assets (Billion RMB)	Total Retail Sales of Consumer Goods (Billion RMB)	Total Volume of Imports and Exports (Billion USD)	Actual Utilized Foreign Capital (Billion USD)
Guangzhou	911.28	265.99	364.78	76.74	3.77
Shenzhen	820.12	170.92	259.87	270.16	4.16
Zhuhai	103.77	41.05	41.38	37.44	1.18
Foshan	481.45	147.06	142.91	38.34	1.87
Jiangmen	135.53	49.21	57.43	11.04	1.04
Dongguan	376.33	109.41	95.63	94.16	2.59
Zhongshan	156.44	54.56	55.48	24.47	0.77
Huizhou	141.04	75.90	50.31	29.24	1.39
Zhaoqing	84.63	46.28	27.58	3.38	0.89
Pearl River Delta total	3,210.59	960.38	1,095.37	584.97	17.66
National total	33,535	22,485	12,534	2,207	90
Percentage of national total	9.6%	4.3%	8.7%	26.5%	19.6%

Source: Compiled from the *Yearbook of Guangdong Province Statistics* (2009), the *2009 Statistics Bulletin of National Economic and Social Development* of nine cities in the Pearl River Delta, and related data in government working reports.

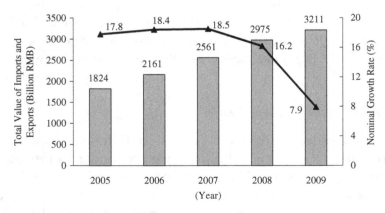

Figure 4.5　Change in Total Value of Imports and Exports in the Pearl River Delta for 2005–2009

Table 4.12   GDP Composition by Industry for the Pearl River Delta for 2004–2009 (Unit: Billion RMB)

Year	Item	GDP of Region	Primary Industry	Secondary Industry Total Value	Secondary Industry Industrial	Tertiary Industry
2004	Total value	1,548.54	55.45	765.04	708.09	728.05
	Rate (%)	100	3.6	49.4	45.7	47.0
2005	Total value	1,824.45	57.48	923.01	862.83	843.96
	Rate (%)	100	3.2	50.6	47.3	46.3
2006	Total value	2,160.86	56.78	1,111.08	1,046.10	993.01
	Rate (%)	100	2.6	51.4	48.4	46.0
2007	Total value	2,560.69	62.54	1,304.68	1,234.12	1,193.47
	Rate (%)	100	2.4	51.0	48.2	46.6
2008	Total value	2,974.56	71.15	1,496.46	1,416.86	1,406.95
	Rate (%)	100	2.4	50.3	47.6	47.3
2009	Total value	3,210.6	73.8	1,534.7	—	1,602.1
	Rate (%)	100	2.3	47.8	—	49.9

Source: Compiled from the *Yearbook of Guangdong Province Statistics* (2009), the *2009 Statistics Bulletin of National Economic and Social Development* of nine cities of the Pearl River Delta, and related data in government working reports.

values of the primary, secondary and tertiary industries of the Delta in 2009 increased by 4.2%, 7.5% and 11.8% respectively, compared with those in 2008, and their percentages in the economy are respectively 2.3%, 47.8% and 49.9%, as shown in Table 4.12.

The export-based manufacturing industry of the Pearl River Delta occupies an important position in China, and even in the world. Many industries with competitive advantages have been established in the region, e.g., transportation equipment, electrical machinery and equipment, communication equipment, computer and other electronic equipment, instruments, and cultural and office-based machinery. The added value of industrial enterprises above the designated size[7] in the Pearl River Delta in 2009 was 1.35 trillion RMB, 9.6% down compared with that in 2008. Table 4.13 shows the details.

---

[7] Industrial enterprises above the designated size are those with annual revenue from principal business over 5 million RMB.

Table 4.13　Added Value of Industrial Enterprises Above the Designated Size[8] in the Pearl River Delta for 2005–2009 (Unit: Billion RMB)

Year Region	2005	2006	2007	2008	2009
Guangzhou	165.40	197.09	241.08	298.77	293.85
Shenzhen	257.20	308.66	329.86	420.72	342.99
Zhuhai	32.87	41.50	47.53	51.66	47.86
Foshan	130.33	174.43	233.25	302.73	286.50
Jiangmen	35.51	43.92	57.64	71.25	70.08
Dongguan	106.05	131.86	143.06	168.90	132.60
Zhongshan	55.12	69.55	82.50	95.40	89.24
Huizhou	31.53	40.42	50.25	61.47	60.60
Zhaoqing	7.69	11.38	16.81	24.48	27.75
Pearl River Delta total	821.70	1,018.81	1,201.98	1,495.37	1,351.47
Nominal growth rate (%)	26.2	24.0	18.0	24.4	−9.6

Source: Compiled from the *Yearbook of Guangdong Province Statistics* (2009) and related data on economic indices of the Pearl River Delta in December 2009.

Import and export trade

The Pearl River Delta is developing into the largest processing trade zone in the world, featuring a huge import and export value and a small ordinary trade value, and the majority of the trade value being of the "three-plus-one" (trading mix: three processing modes and one complement trade) type. The total import and export value of the Pearl River Delta in 2009 was 584.97 billion USD, accounting for 26.5% of the national amount. Although its total volume decreased for the first time in recent years due to the impact of the global financial crisis (see Figure 4.6), the magnitude of decline narrowed month by month during 2009. The total export value of the Pearl River Delta in 2009 was 341.78 billion USD, 11.7% down compared with that in 2008; export products mainly were mechanical, electrical and high-tech products.

---

[8] Industrial enterprises above the designated size are those with annual revenue from principal business over 5 million RMB.

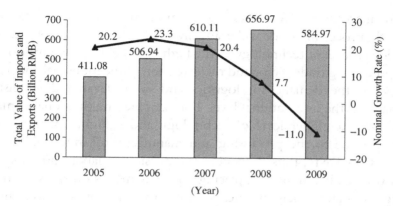

Figure 4.6 Changes in Total Import and Export Value of the Pearl River Delta for 2005–2009

Source: Compiled from the *Yearbook of Guangdong Province Statistics* (2009), the *2009 Statistics Bulletin of National Economic and Social Development* of nine cities in the Pearl River Delta, and related data in government working reports.

4.3.2 *Main Characteristics of the Development of Logistics in the Pearl River Delta*

Logistics for the manufacturing industry and the transition of the processing trade sector

The Pearl River Delta has already become a global base for processing and manufacturing industries and has formed two industry clusters: an electronic information industry led by Shenzhen, Dongguan and Huizhou and an electrical appliance industry led by Guangzhou, Foshan, Jiangmen and Zhuhai. It has attracted many multinational companies and well-known domestic enterprises to set up factories in the region, creating tremendous demand for the logistics industry therein. Processing trade has become a prominent feature of the export-based economy of the Delta; the massive scale of processing trade and the "three-plus-one" processing format highlight the important role logistics-related industries play in the supply chain of the manufacturing industry in this region.

Through many years of development, the Pearl River Delta has entered the acceleration stage of economic and social transition: the regional economy will see a change from extensive growth to intensive growth; processing trade will gradually change from simple processing at a lower level of technology to the high-tech fields. The transition of the processing trade sector and the extension of the industrial chain has propelled the demand for logistics and even elevated the logistics demand to the international level. For example, multinational companies bring a higher level of technology and a higher potential for adding value to the processing and manufacturing industries in the Pearl River Delta, thus deepening the division of labor and cooperation with global industries, placing higher demands on specialization, integration and timely logistics services in this region and even international logistics services. The exported finished products of processing trade have changed from traditional bulky products with low value to high-tech miniature products with high value, generating higher demand for refined logistics.

Impact of the financial crisis on the growth of logistics demand

The high level of export orientation and the rapid economic growth had led to tremendous demand for logistics in the Pearl River Delta. Yet due to the spread of the international financial crisis and its impact on economic entities as well as the underlying structural discord, the economy of the Pearl River Delta has been affected seriously and thus the consistent growth trend of logistics demand therein was devastated in recent years. In 2009, the total cargo transport volume (1.33 billion tons) and total transit volume (403.28 billion ton-km) of the Delta both decreased slightly compared to that in 2008, as shown in Tables 4.14 and 4.15.

Logistics integration and cooperation with Hong Kong and Macao

The Pearl River Delta is endowed with a convenient multi-mode transportation network and a massive economic base; all cities in the region are connected into a close unit by the Pearl River, as well as the Beijing-Guangzhou and Beijing-Kowloon Railways and Highways. By the end of 2008, the highway mileage of the Delta was 53,418 km

Table 4.14   Status of Cargo Transport in the Pearl River Delta in 2009

Region	Cargo Transportation (Million Tons)	Freight Flows (Billion Ton-km)	Port Cargo Throughput (Million Tons)	Container Throughput at Port (Million TEUs)	Airport Cargo Throughput (1,000 Tons)
Guangzhou	525.16	218.49	375.61	11.30	1,221.9
Shenzhen	223.68	113.66	193.65	18.25	605.4
Zhuhai	66.82	14.85	44.07	0.56	13.8
Foshan	178.02	16.83	50.99	—	—
Jiangmen	66.91	7.57	41.70	—	—
Dongguan	87.33	10.17	35.30	—	—
Zhongshan	69.91*	5.86	34.02	—	—
Huizhou	84.13	12.54	37.88	0.19	—
Zhaoqing	26.47	3.31	11.29	0.35	—
Pearl River Delta total	1,328.43#	403.28	824.51	35.45#	—
National total	27,880	12,121	6,910	121	—
Percentage of national total	4.8%#	3.3%	11.9%	29.3%	—

Note: Data marked with "*" are taken from 2008 statistics; data marked with "#" are estimated values.

Source: Compiled from the *Statistical Bulletin of National Economic and Social Development* (2009) and related data compiled from websites on statistical information of nine municipal governments of the Pearl River Delta.

Table 4.15   Changes in Total Freight Traffic and Freight Flows of the Pearl River Delta for 2005–2009

Item	2005	2006	2007	2008	2009
Total freight traffic (million tons)	1,033.65	1,132.75	1,224.08	1,340.21	1,328.43#
Freight flows (billion ton-km)	361.03	381.58	407.63	403.42	403.28

Note: Data marked with "#" are estimated values.

Source: Compiled from the *Yearbook of Guangdong Province Statistics* (2009) and related data compiled from websites on statistical information of nine municipal governments of the Pearl River Delta.

and the number of freight trucks reached 939,400. Presently, the Pearl River Delta has formed a railway network with hubs in Guangzhou and Shenzhen, a port system with the Pearl River Delta sharing loads with Hong Kong, a hub airport centered at Guangzhou Baiyun International Airport, with branch airports consisting of Shenzhen, Zhuhai, Foshan Airports, and a civil aviation transportation system collaborating with Hong Kong and Macao Airports.

At the end of 2008, China's State Council approved the *Outline for the Plan for the Reform and Development of the Pearl River Delta (2008–2020)*, dictating essentially the construction of vital infrastructure between the Pearl River Delta, Hong Kong and Macao. The plan directs the construction of the Hong Kong-Zhuhai-Macao Bridge, the Shenzhen Eastern Channel and the Guangzhou-Shenzhen-Hong Kong Express Railway, to constitute an integrated and comprehensive traffic and transport system closely connecting Hong Kong, Macao and the Pearl River Delta.

Ports as important strategic resources for regional logistics development

The Pearl River Delta has a relatively prominent port economy. As a key node for comprehensive transportation, ports are one of the platforms connecting the Pearl River Delta with other domestic and international markets. They are the gathering pool of logistics, business and information, playing an important role in the comprehensive logistics system therein, being an important strategic resource for the development of modern logistics in the area and the main engine in propelling the logistics development in this region. In 2009, throughput at ports of the Pearl River Delta was 824.51 million tons, 2.0% up compared with that in 2008 and accounting for 11.9% of the national total; its container throughput was 35.45 million TEUs, accounting for 29.3% of the national total.

The extensive river network of the Pearl River Delta connects Guangzhou Port and Shenzhen Port with more than ten inland small ports and provides the Delta with the most convenient water transportation channel, constituting a port cluster system with Guangzhou

Port and Shenzhen Port[9] as the centers, and Zhuhai, Zhongshan, Humen and Huizhou Ports as artery ports and feeder ports. Guangzhou Port is a comprehensive main hub port of Southern China, and a main transshipment port for energy and raw material for the Pearl River Delta, while Shenzhen Port is a main trade port for container transportation for China.

Internationalization and competition of logistics enterprises

The Pearl River Delta is the center of global manufacturing; the development levels of its manufacturing enterprises and the corresponding logistics service matching are both high. While regional trade has made the transition to export-based deep processing and auxiliary service industries, the relationship between the Pearl River Delta and the foreign economy has become much closer than before, manifesting an obvious trend of internationalization in the development of its logistics enterprises. Founded on an export-based economy and a concentration of relatively advanced transportation/storage industries, the logistics industry in the Pearl River Delta started on high ground and has evolved rapidly to be in the forefront in China. Many large-scale multinational logistics enterprises have also swarmed into the Pearl River Delta, stirring up fierce competition in the logistics market.

By the end of 2008, there were 11,561 transportation and storage enterprises and 576,600 practitioners in the Pearl River Delta; among them 8,570 transportation and storage firms were in Guangzhou and Shenzhen, accounting for 74.1% of the total number in the region. Table 4.16 shows the details.

Domestic and foreign demand driving the development of logistics

Currently, the Pearl River Delta faces significant opportunities for development. First, the global industries will continue to shift into

---

[9] Both Guangzhou Port and Shenzhen Port ranked among the world's top ten container ports in 2009.

Table 4.16   Transportation and Storage Industries of the Pearl River Delta in 2008

Region	Number of Enterprises (Units)	Number of Practitioners (1,000 Persons)	Total Assets (Billion RMB)	Income of Main Business (Billion RMB)	Profit of Business (Billion RMB)
Guangzhou	4,398	322.8	321.18	146.09	13.60
Shenzhen	4,172	—	—	85.21	9.16*
Zhuhai	536	21.8	18.36	5.88	0.25
Foshan	—	—	—	—	—
Jiangmen	255	15.5	6.05	3.99	0.94
Dongguan	803	35.3	26.54	8.77	2.00
Zhongshan	285	17.9	7.79	3.16	0.75
Huizhou	412	19.7	13.90	6.00	1.93
Zhaoqing	199	8.8	2.53	1.52	0.31
Pearl River Delta total	11,561#	576.6#	—	—	—
Guangdong Province	13,644	817.7	—	—	—
National total	143,902	10,177	—	—	—
Pearl River Delta total as percentage of national total	8.0%#	5.7%#	—	—	—

Note: Data marked with "*" do not include data for storage industry; data marked with "#" are estimated values.

Source: Compiled from the 2008 Second National Economic Census of nine cities in the Pearl River Delta.

the Asia-Pacific region; economic cooperation and communication in the Asia-Pacific region as well as the progress of the China-ASEAN Free Trade Area will be sped up. Second, as China is still at a stage with significant strategic opportunity. With the implementation of the Closer Economic Partnership Arrangement (CEPA), the Pearl River Delta has become the bridge of trade cooperation between Hong Kong-Macao and the Mainland, and afforded a greater development potential in regional cooperation. Meanwhile, the Pearl River Delta covers a massive area and is endowed with an advanced waterway and land transportation network, spreading across neighboring regions of several provinces, districts and cities. These provinces, districts and cities are engaged in import and export trade, relying on the Pearl River Delta as a transit point, so the demand for cross-district logistics will have a broader stage for development. Through 30 years of reform and opening-up, the Pearl River Delta has accumulated a solid base of material resources; its economic strength and regional competitiveness have also been notably improved. The logistics of the Pearl River Delta features a two-pronged force of domestic and foreign demand, which provides favorable conditions for further development of the regional logistics industry.

4.4 Development Status of Logistics in the Bohai Rim Region

The Bohai Rim Region includes three provinces (Shandong, Hebei, Liaoning) and two municipalities (Beijing, Tianjin), occupying a total area of 522,000 km^2, accounting for 5.4% of China's territory. The total population of the Bohai Rim Region was approximately 238 million, accounting for 17.84% of the total national population, by the end of 2009. The Region, located at the junction of three geographical zones, i.e., North China, Northeast China and East China, is one of the densest areas of urban clusters, harbor clusters and industrial clusters in China. It is also situated in the heartland of the Northeast Asia economic region, which is an important channel for Northern China to the Pacific Ocean and the rest of the world, and holds an irreplaceable position in the economic development of Northern China. Since entering the 21st century, the Bohai Rim Region showed an even stronger pace of growth, gradually becoming the third pole after the Pearl River Delta and Yangtze River Delta in advancing China's economic growth, and is one of the most dynamic economic regions in China.

4.4.1   Overview of Economic Development in the Bohai Rim Region

Regional economic output

In 2009, the Bohai Rim Region achieved rapid economic development, as regional GDP reached 8,526.5 billion RMB, 9.92%[10] up compared with that in 2008. In view of GDP growth, Beijing, Tianjin and Liaoning increased by 13.14%, 18.04% and 11.92% respectively, higher than the national average level, while the growth rates of Hebei and Shandong lagged behind the national level, as shown in Table 4.17.

Industrial structure

In 2009, the industrial added values of the primary, secondary and tertiary industries in the Bohai Rim Region were 711.0 billion RMB, 4,258.5 billion RMB and 3,556.9 billion RMB respectively, increasing

Table 4.17   GDP and Growth Rate in the Bohai Rim Region for 2008–2009

Province/Municipality	GDP (Billion RMB)		Nominal Growth Rate
	2008	2009	
Beijing	1,048.8	1,186.6	13.14%
Tianjin	635.4	750.1	18.04%
Hebei	1,618.9	1,702.7	5.18%
Liaoning	1,346.2	1,506.6	11.92%
Shandong	3,107.2	3,380.5	8.80%
Bohai Rim Region total	7,756.5	8,526.5	9.92%

Source: Compiled from the *China Statistical Yearbook* (2009) and the *2009 Statistical Bulletin of National Economic and Social Development* of Beijing, Tianjin, Hebei Province, Liaoning Province and Shandong Province, published by the National Bureau of Statistics of China.

---

[10] In this chapter, the growth rates of GDP, total agricultural output value, industrial added value and the total value of imports and exports are nominal rates unless otherwise stated, i.e., the calculation does not take into account the factor of price changes.

Table 4.18   Industrial Structure in the Bohai Rim Region, 2009

	Beijing	Tianjin	Hebei	Liaoning	Shandong
Primary industry (%)	1.00	1.75	13.04	9.39	9.54
Secondary industry (%)	23.12	54.80	52.12	51.92	56.31
Tertiary industry (%)	75.88	43.45	34.84	38.69	34.15

Source: Compiled from the *China Statistical Yearbook* (2009) and the *2009 Statistical Bulletin of National Economic and Social Development* of Beijing, Tianjin, Hebei Province, Liaoning Province and Shandong Province, published by the National Bureau of Statistics of China.

by 8.14%, 5.13% and 16.68% compared to that in 2008. The percentages of added value in regional GDP for the three industries were respectively 8.34%, 49.95% and 41.71%. The industrial structure for the region exhibits a "II, III, I" pattern, as the secondary and tertiary industries prevailed, except for Beijing which has a "III, II, I" pattern, as shown in Table 4.18.

The Bohai Rim Region possesses a solid industrial foundation and is China's industrial base for heavy and chemical industries. Liaoning Anshan Iron and Steel Company and Beijing Capital Iron and Steel Company are large-scale steel enterprises; Beijing Yanshan Petrochemical Group and Tianjin Bohai Chemical Industry Group are the premier large-scale nationwide chemical enterprises; Shenyang's heavy machinery and precision machine tool manufacturing industry, Beijing's and Tianjin's electronic product and automobile manufacturing industries and Shijiazhuang's cotton industry all hold important positions in China. The industrial structure of the Bohai Rim Region also has some distinct attributes, as Beijing, Tianjin and Shandong principally have the light industries and high-technology industries, while Hebei and Liaoning focus mainly on heavy and chemical industries.

Status of import and export trade

Affected by the global financial crisis, the 2009 gross value of imports and exports was 509.8 billion USD (Table 4.19) in the Bohai Rim Region,

Table 4.19   Import and Export Trade of Provinces/Municipalities in the Bohai Rim Region for 2008–2009

Province/Municipality	Total Import and Export Value (Billion USD)		Nominal Growth Rate
	2008	2009	
Beijing	271.7	214.8	−20.9%
Tianjin	80.4	63.9	−20.6%
Hebei	38.4	29.6	−22.9%
Liaoning	72.4	62.9	−13.1%
Shandong	158.4	138.6	−12.4%
Bohai Rim Region total	621.3	509.8	−18.0%

Source: Compiled from the *2009 Statistical Bulletin of National Economic and Social Development* of Beijing, Tianjin, Hebei Province, Liaoning Province and Shandong Province, published by the National Bureau of Statistics of China.

18.0% lower than that in 2008, with the gross export value falling sharply in particular. For instance, the export value of Hebei Province in 2009 was 15.7 billion USD, down 34.6% compared with that in 2008.

During 2009, the proportions of electromechanical and high-tech products in the total value of exports in the Bohai Rim Region increased continually. For example, the proportions of electromechanical and high-tech products in the total value of exports of Shandong in 2009 were 43.0% and 17.2% respectively, increasing by 1.8% and 2.5% compared with that in 2008. For Tianjin, the export values of electromechanical and high-tech products were 20.5 billion USD and 11.9 billion USD, accounting for 68.2% and 39.8% of the city's total export value, and increased by 6.1% and 4.5% respectively from that in 2008.

4.4.2 Main Characteristics of the Logistics Development in the Bohai Rim Region

Accelerated development of the modern logistics industry

The Bohai Rim Region, having the advantage of being located at the junction of three geographical zones, is one of the key marine gateways for Northern China to the Asia-Pacific region and the rest of the world. Along with the gradual development of its transportation network in recent years, all kinds of transportation modes and communication networks have been substantially upgraded and modernized, and modern logistics infrastructures have also made remarkable headway.

In recent years, logistics delegates, multinational companies and consulting agencies from the United States, Japan, Germany and South Korea frequently visited the major cities in the Bohai Rim Region, bringing with them prosperous exchanges and cooperation. FedEx, UPS and other world-renowned multinational logistics companies have settled in Tianjin, Dalian and other large cities. Conventional transportation and storage companies are being transformed and upgraded to modern modes of logistics; third- and fourth-party logistics enterprises are developing rapidly as well.

Significant enhancement of the competitive advantages of port logistics

Owning to its many ports and their wide coverage of the hinterland, the Bohai Rim Region is an important marine outfall for regions like Northeast China, North China, Northwest China and West China. Presently, there are 12 major ports rendering container transportation services, namely Dalian, Yingkou, Jinzhou and Dandong of Liaoning Province; Qingdao, Yantai, Weihai, Rizhao and Longkou of Shandong Province; Qinhuangdao and Jingtang of Hebei Province; as well as Tianjin Port. Among them, Tianjin Port handled 380 million tons of cargo throughput in 2009, ranking No. 5 in the world; it recorded 8.7 million TEUs of container throughput, ranking No. 11 in the world. Currently, Tianjin Port has become a world-class manmade deepwater port, and the largest comprehensive port in North China.

The cargo throughputs of major ports in the Bohai Rim Region since 2005 are shown in Table 4.20.

Table 4.20   Cargo Throughput of Ports Above the Designated Size[11] in the Bohai Rim Region for 2005–2008 (Unit: Million Tons)

Ports	2005	2006	2007	2008
Dalian	170.85	200.46	222.86	245.88
Yingkou	75.37	94.77	122.07	150.85
Qinhuangdao	169.00	204.89	248.93	252.31
Tianjin	240.69	257.60	309.46	355.93
Yantai	45.06	60.76	101.29	111.89
Qingdao	186.78	224.15	265.02	300.29
Rizhao	84.21	110.07	130.63	151.02
Bohai Rim Region total	971.96	1,152.70	1,400.26	1,568.17

Source: Compiled from the *China Statistical Yearbook* (2008–2009), published by the National Bureau of Statistics of China.

Role of logistics parks in regional logistics development

Beijing has become one of the largest distribution centers of goods and an import-based international procurement center in China. Currently there are four logistics centers in Beijing, i.e., Tianzhu and Shibalidian in Chaoyang District northeast of the city, Daxing to the south and Menkougou to the west. These four logistics centers together with the urban logistics center form the framework of Beijing's logistics network.

In recent years, Tianjin initiated 12 key logistics park projects one after another, e.g., Tianjin Port Bulk Cargo Logistics Center, Tianjin Container Logistics Center, Tianjin Bonded Logistics Park, Tianjin International Airport Logistics Zone, Tianjin Logistics Freight Center and Postal Logistics Center. Tianjin Bonded Logistics Park, established in August 2004, has now become the largest logistics center in Northern China.

---

[11] Ports above the designated size include seaports with over 1 million tons of annual throughput capacity, river ports with over 2 million tons of annual throughput capacity and ports which handle foreign trade and container business, as specified by the Ministry of Transport.

In 2009, the other provinces of the Bohai Rim Region had also made notable progress in the construction of logistics parks. For example, Hebei Province had charted out ten large-scale logistics parks such as Provincial Postal Logistics Park, Provincial Transportation Logistics Park, Shijiazhuang International Logistics Park, Shijiazhuang Aviation Logistics Park, and Tangshan Port Energy Raw Materials Logistics Park. Shandong Province had begun to construct the nation's largest distribution center of agricultural products — Shouguang Agricultural Logistics Park. In 2009, Liaoning Province attained progressive success in promoting the construction of logistics facilities, e.g., Northeast Asia Logistics Park, Shenhai Integrated Logistics Park, Shenxi Industry Logistics Park, Shenbei Integrated Logistics Park, Shutao Road Logistics Belt, Tiexi Steel Logistics, Automotive Trade Concentrated Zone, and Hunnan Comprehensive Logistics Park.

Shenyang Bonded Logistics Center was one of the top 50 logistics parks in China. In February 2009, it was granted approval by the General Administration of Customs, the Ministry of Finance, State Administration of Taxation and State Administration of Foreign Exchange and officially became one of the pilot expansion units of the 23 domestic bonded logistics centers. This was the only bonded logistics center in the inland areas of the three provinces in Northeast China, with a planned area of 10 km^2 and a total investment of 500 million RMB. On October 13, 2009, it officially began operation.[12]

Trend for multipolar development of the regional logistics industry

Different from the unipolar logistics structure such as that in the Pearl River Delta with Hong Kong as the center, or the Yangtze River Delta with Shanghai as the center, the development of the logistics industry in the Bohai Rim Region leans toward a multipolar trend. For example, Liaodong Peninsula with Dalian as the core, Jiaodong Peninsula

---

[12] "Shenyang Bonded Logistics Center is honored as one of the top 50 logistics parks in China", Huanbohai News, November 26, 2009. http://huanbohai.huanbohainews. com.cn/system/2009/11/26/010523656.shtml.

with Qingdao as the core and Tianjin city all have the potential to develop into the logistics centers of the region, and all have proposed a similar policy goal.

Currently, none of the cities have the definite advantage to lead the development of regional logistics in the Bohai Rim Region. All cities have proposed plans to "invigorate the city through the harbor", and accelerate the development of port resources. Besides the big four ports in Dalian, Qinhuangdao, Tianjin and Qingdao, there are many other ports emerging quickly in the Bohai Bay, including Yingkou Port, Yantai Port, Rizhao Port, Dandong Port, Jinzhou Port, Jingtang Port, Longkou Port and Weihai Port.

Judging from the economic development perspective, an intra-regional industrial division of labor and cooperation system within the Bohai Rim Region has not been formed. Mutual collaboration and economic integration of industries are still lacking. Among the three major regions, the metropolitan areas of Beijing/Tianjin and Hebei, Liaodong Peninsula and Shandong Peninsula, economic activities are relatively independent; industrial convergence among the three provinces and two municipalities is prominent, yet horizontal ties among enterprises are fewer; the export-oriented economic development of the Bohai Rim is also relatively slow.

Industry linkages enhance logistics operational efficiency

The Bohai Rim Region possesses a solid industrial foundation and is China's industrial base for heavy and chemical industries. Manufactured goods account for a great part of the total logistics business; and stable development of the manufacturing industries makes a significant contribution to the modern logistics industry. The provinces/municipalities of the Bohai Rim Region all attach great importance to the joint development between the logistics industry and other industries. For example, in order to promote the joint development of the logistics and manufacturing industries, Shenyang city has taken a series of measures to optimize the environment for interactive development, including the construction of an integrated service platform and an information platform for manufacturing and logistics companies, and creating a good public service environment for joint development. Shandong, Hebei and other provinces have also instituted development plans for linking the two industries. Promoting the joint development of the manufacturing and logistics industries in the Bohai Rim Region is not only beneficial in resolving the negative effects of the current financial crisis, but is also conducive to speeding up the pace of upgrading the regional modern manufacturing industries, to fostering a modern logistics system, and to laying a solid foundation for future economic development.

Impact of the financial crisis on the regional logistics industry

The global financial crisis has greatly affected the overall logistics industry in the Bohai Rim Region, but the impact within the logistics industry is quite different. The direct impact of the financial crisis was mainly reflected in the decline of total external logistics demand, among which the shipping, ports and international freight forwarding logistics industries were affected most conspicuously. For example, the three major hub ports, Tianjin, Dalian and Qingdao, respectively had cargo throughputs of 355.9 million tons, 246 million tons and 300.3 million tons in 2008, of which foreign trade throughputs were 204.6 million tons, 86 million tons and 206.6 million tons. Comparing with that in 2007, cargo throughputs decreased by 5.1%, 0.9% and 4.95% respectively, while foreign trade throughputs decreased by 17.5%, 12.7% and 4.28% respectively. The three major ports had an annual container throughput of 8.502 million TEUs, 4.525 million TEUs and 10.377 million TEUs, respectively. Comparing with 2007, Tianjin gained slightly but Dalian and Qingdao decreased by 0.1% and 12.63% respectively.

As for logistics enterprises, those with traditional and singular logistics services were less risk-resilient, so they were affected by the financial crisis more seriously; on the other hand, modern logistics enterprises and logistics companies with integrated logistics services were less affected. In addition, due to the slow recovery of the world economy, the international logistics market continues to suffer from the impact, and the international logistics businesses are obviously affected. Meanwhile, due to the Government's policy of expanding domestic demand, domestic consumption is quite strong and therefore logistics companies which focus on domestic logistics businesses are less affected.

4.5 Development Status of Logistics in Hong Kong and Taiwan

Hong Kong, Taiwan and the Mainland have a close relationship in terms of their history, culture, politics and economy. Located on the southeastern side of China, Hong Kong has a fine natural deepwater port and a large-scale international airport, and its logistics industry is one of the four pillar industries of the Hong Kong economy. Located in the central Asia-Pacific region, Taiwan has an island-based economy, with confined land and a dense population.

4.5.1 *Economic Development Status of Hong Kong and Taiwan*

Economic status of Hong Kong

Hong Kong's GDP in 2009 was 1.63 trillion HKD (210.6 billion USD),[13] 2.6% down compared with that in 2008. This was the first time the figure had declined since the 1998 financial crisis of Southeast Asia, as shown in Figure 4.7. Compared with that in the same period in 2008, the decline of the first three quarters reduced gradually, before the growth rate rose to 2.7% in the fourth quarter. The GDP of Hong Kong was expected to increase by 4–5% in 2010.

The foreign trade of Hong Kong in 2009 was 5.16 trillion HKD, 11.8% down compared with that in 2008. This was the first time it had decreased since 2001. Furthermore, its export, import and transshipment trades all showed a decline, as seen in Table 4.21. The service trade of Hong Kong in 2009 decreased by 6.7%. Export

---

[13] The average exchange rate of the Hong Kong dollar in 2009 was 7.752 HKD to 1 USD according to the 2010 Hong Kong Statistical Figures Chart.

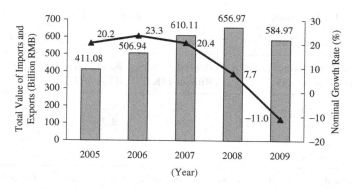

Figure 4.7 Changes in GDP of Hong Kong for 2005–2009

Source: Compiled from the Statistics Department of the Government of Hong Kong Special Administrative Region, May 14, 2010.

Table 4.21 Foreign Trade and Growth Rate of Hong Kong for 2005–2009 (Unit: Billion HKD)

Item	2005	2006	2007	2008	2009 Total Value	2009 Growth Rate (%)
Import (CIF)	2,329.47	2,599.80	2,868.01	3,025.29	2,692.36	−11.0
Export (FOB)	2,250.17	2,461.03	2,687.51	2,824.15	2,469.09	−12.6
Export of Hong Kong products	136.03	134.53	109.12	90.76	57.74	−36.4
Transshipment	2,114.14	2,326.50	2,578.39	2,733.39	2,411.35	−11.8
Balance of trade	−79.30	−138.78	−180.50	−201.14	−223.27	—
Total trade value	4,579.64	5,060.83	5,555.52	5,849.44	5,161.45	−11.8

Source: Compiled from related data published by the Statistics Department of the Government of Hong Kong Special Administrative Region, May 27, 2010.

services relating to transportation, finance and trading business, which had seen rapid growth in recent years, all declined; among these, export of transportation services experienced the highest decrease of 13.6%.

Table 4.22   Change in Industrial Structure of Hong Kong for 2005–2008

Year	Primary Industry		Secondary Industry		Tertiary Industry	
	Added Value (Billion HKD)	Rate (%)	Added Value (Billion HKD)	Rate (%)	Added Value (Billion HKD)	Rate (%)
2005	0.85	0.1	124.11	9.3	1,207.87	90.6
2006	0.85	0.1	124.91	8.7	1,297.55	91.2
2007	0.90	0.1	119.26	7.7	1,431.82	92.3
2008	0.82	0.1	125.15	8.1	1,441.93	92.0

Source: Compiled from related data published by the Statistics Department of the Government of Hong Kong Special Administrative Region.

Table 4.23   Annual Changes in GDP Among Various Industries of Hong Kong for 2008–2009 (Unit: %)

Project	2008	2009
Manufacturing industry	−6.6	−9.2
Construction industry	8.8	1.6
Service industry	2.5	−2.0
Wholesale and retail	4.2	−3.5
Trade industry of import and export	7.2	−8.9
Transportation and storage industries	2.1	−6.5
Finance and insurance industry	−1.3	1.9

Source: Compiled from the *The First Quarter Economic Report* (2010), published by the Financial Secretary of the Hong Kong Special Administrative Region, May 2010.

From 2005 to 2008, the added value of Hong Kong's tertiary industry, led by service industries such as trade, transportation, finance and insurance industries, rose continually, accounting for more than 90% of the total GDP of Hong Kong, as shown in Table 4.22. In 2009, the net value of the service industry of Hong Kong decreased by 2%, among which the transportation and storage industries decreased by 6.5% in the year, as seen in Table 4.23.

Economic status of Taiwan

The GDP of Taiwan in 2009 was 12.51 trillion NTD (379 billion USD),[14] 1.9%[15] down compared with that in 2008. In 2009, the decline of the first three quarters reduced gradually, before the growth rate rose to 9.1% in the fourth quarter. Taiwan's GDP was expected to increase by 6.14% in 2010.

In 2009, the total value of foreign trade in Taiwan was 378.05 billion USD, 23.8% down compared with that in 2008, decreasing for the first time since 2001; the import and export values decreased by 20.3% and 27.5% respectively. Due to the drastic decrease in imports, the trade surplus climbed to a new historical high of 29.3 billion USD. The value of export orders in 2009 was 322.43 billion USD, 8.3% down compared with that in 2008, as shown in Table 4.24.

Mainland China, Hong Kong and Macao together have become the largest export region for Taiwan, as well as its second-largest import source. In recent years, the proportion of trade value with the

Table 4.24 Status of Foreign Trade of Taiwan for 2005–2009 (Unit: Billion USD)

Year	Export Value	Import Value	Difference	Export Value	Import Value	Growth Value	Rate (%)
	Trade Balance			**Growth Rate (%)**		**Export Order**	
2005	198.43	182.61	15.82	8.8	8.2	256.40	19.2
2006	224.02	202.70	21.32	12.9	11.0	299.31	16.7
2007	246.68	219.25	27.43	10.1	8.2	345.81	15.5
2008	255.63	240.45	15.18	3.6	9.7	351.73	1.7
2009	203.68	174.37	29.30	−20.3	−27.5	322.43	−8.3

Source: Compiled from related data published by the Statistics Department of Taiwan Ministry of Economy, May 28, 2010.

---

[14] The average exchange rate of the New Taiwan dollar in 2009 was 33 NTD to 1 USD, according to data published by the Taiwan Ministry of Economy.
[15] Real growth rate (in terms of fixed price of 2006).

Mainland, Hong Kong and Macao in Taiwan's total foreign trade value has increased continually. The total trade value of Taiwan with the Mainland, Hong Kong and Macao in 2009, as shown in Table 4.25, was 109.56 billion USD, 17.6% down compared with that in 2008, and accounting for 29% of the total amount of foreign trade in Taiwan.

Taiwan's economic structure had made the transition from an agriculture-based economy to an industry-based economy and then to a chiefly service-based economy. In recent years, along with the rapid development of the service industry, the percentages of GDP for agriculture and industry in total GDP have decreased slightly. In 2009, the GDP of the service industry accounted for 68.66% of total GDP, while the GDP of industry accounted for 29.79% of the total amount (of which the GDP of manufacturing industry accounted for 24.67%). Table 4.26 shows the details.

4.5.2 *Development Status of the Logistics Industry in Hong Kong and Taiwan*

Development status of the logistics industry in Hong Kong

Hong Kong possesses a world-class container port, with its through-put ranking No. 3 among global container ports, and shipping lines spreading all over the world. By the end of 2009, the number of ships registered in Hong Kong was 1,496, 9.9% up compared with that in 2008; among which the number of ocean steamers was 1,266, accounting for 84.6% of the total. Hong Kong International Airport is one of the most important multi-modal logistics hubs in China, with 800 take-offs and landings daily. In 2009 Hong Kong had 2,050 km of public highway, 107,000 freight trucks and a railway network with a total length of over 170 km.

In 2009, the total freight traffic of Hong Kong was 274.34 million tons, 7% down compared with that in 2008, which was also the first time it had declined since the Southeast Asian financial crisis. The total freight traffic of various transportation means are shown in Table 4.27. The cargo throughput at ports for the year was

Table 4.25 Statistics of Taiwan's Trade with the Mainland, Hong Kong and Macao (Unit: Billion USD)

Year	Total Trade Value			Export Value			Import Value			Trade Balance
	Value	Growth Rate (%)	Proportion (%)	Value	Growth Rate (%)	Proportion (%)	Value	Growth Rate (%)	Proportion (%)	
2005	100.24	13.0	26.3	78.00	12.1	39.3	22.24	16.2	12.2	55.77
2006	116.14	15.9	27.2	89.45	14.7	39.9	26.69	20.0	13.2	62.76
2007	130.64	12.5	28.0	100.78	12.7	40.9	29.87	11.9	13.6	70.91
2008	132.89	1.7	26.8	99.98	-0.8	39.1	32.91	10.2	13.7	67.06
2009	109.56	-17.6	29.0	84.00	-16.0	41.2	25.56	-22.3	14.7	58.44

Source: Compiled from related data published by the National Trade Bureau of Taiwan Ministry of Economy, May 26, 2009.

Table 4.26   Industrial Structure of Taiwan for 2005–2009 (Unit: %)

| Year | Agriculture | Industry | | | Service Industry | |
		Total	Manufacturing Industry	Total	Transportation and Storage Industries
2005	1.67	31.26	26.53	67.08	3.52
2006	1.61	31.33	26.46	67.06	3.22
2007	1.49	31.38	26.52	67.12	3.21
2008	1.60	29.25	24.98	69.16	3.15
2009	1.55	29.79	24.67	68.66	3.10*

Note: Data marked with "*" are estimated values.
Source: Compiled from related data published by the Statistics Department of Taiwan Ministry of Economy, May 25, 2010, and data published by the Economic Construction Committee of Taiwan.

Table 4.27   Total Freight Traffic (Import and Export) of Hong Kong for 2005–2009 (Unit: 1,000 Tons)

| Year | Sea Transport | River Transport | Highway Cargo Transport | Railway Cargo Transport | Air Transport | Total | |
						Total Volume	Growth Rate (%)
2005	161,467	68,672	38,719*	215	3,402	272,475	2.9
2006	166,208	72,031	37,320*	184	3,580	279,322	2.5
2007	177,347	68,086	36,139*	141	3,742	285,456	2.2
2008	179,974	79,428	31,734*	109	3,627	294,873	3.3
2009	161,591	81,376	27,939*	84	3,347	274,337	−7.0

Note: Categorical values in this table may not add up to the total value due to rounding up or down; data marked with "*" do not include livestock.
Source: *Hong Kong Port Transportation Statistics Summary*, published by the Hong Kong Port Development Council, May 2010.

242.97 million tons, 6.3% down compared with that in 2008; container throughput at ports was 21.04 million TEUs (among which cargo containers accounted for 17.73 million TEUs), 14.1% down compared with that in 2008, as shown in Figure 4.8.

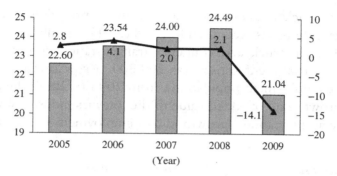

Figure 4.8 Container Throughput and Growth Rate of Hong Kong for 2005–2009

Source: Compiled from the *Hong Kong Port Transportation Statistics Summary*, published by the Hong Kong Port Development Council (2010–2005).

In terms of infrastructure, the Hong Kong-Zhuhai-Macao Bridge[16] began construction in December 2009 as a highway bridge to connect Hong Kong, Zhuhai and Macao, and is expected to begin service around 2015–2016 as planned. The Hong Kong section of the Guangzhou-Shenzhen-Hong Kong high-speed rail was approved for construction in October 2009; it will be connected with the national high-speed railway network and is expected to be in full service in 2014. The construction of the Hong Kong-Zhuhai-Macao Bridge as well as the Hong Kong section of the Guangzhou-Shenzhen-Hong Kong high-speed rail will speed up the all-round cooperation and integration development of Hong Kong, Macao and the Pearl River Delta.

In 2008, the added value of the logistics industry of Hong Kong was 62.1 billion HKD, accounting for 4% of the total regional GDP; the number of logistics enterprises was 12,932,[17] of which the

---

[16] The entire length of the Hong Kong-Zhuhai-Macao Bridge is 49.968 km; it will be the longest cross-ocean bridge in the world when completed.

[17] The Hong Kong Logistics Cargo Transportation Industry Training Committee (managed by the Hong Kong Vocational Training Council) categorizes the logistics industry of Hong Kong into nine types: warehouse and cold storage, freight station, truck and container shipping, air transportation, freight forwarding, ship/dock loading and unloading, international express delivery, other logistics operations and ocean transport.

number of truck and container transportation enterprises and freight forwarder enterprises accounted for 91.8%.[18] The number of employees working in truck and container transportation enterprises and freight forwarding enterprises was 209,300, accounting for 5.9% of the entire employment population. From 2003 to 2008, the average annual growth rate of added value of the logistics industry was 2.3%, while the average annual growth rate of employment was 1.2%.

Development status of the logistics industry in Taiwan

Local cargo transportation in Taiwan in 2009 was 643.89 million tons, which was 3.5% down compared with that in 2008, making it a successive decline for the last two years. Highway cargo transportation accounted for 92.7% of total cargo transportation. Air transportation grew 2.4% whereas cargo transportation of other means all decreased at different levels as shown in Table 4.28.

Among Taiwan's seven international ports, Keelung, Taichung, Kaohsiung and Hualien Ports are the four main ones. Kaohsiung

Table 4.28   Distribution of Local Cargo Transportation in Taiwan for 2005–2009 (Unit: 1,000 Tons)

					2009		
Item	2005	2006	2007	2008	Total Volume	Percent (%)	Growth Rate (%)
Highway	561,831	594,214	617,567	604,137	596,742	92.7	−1.2
Waterway	55,471	53,597	49,642	46,252	32,949	5.1	−28.8
Railway	19,251	19,060	17,378	16,583	14,144	2.2	−14.7
Aviation	55	54	52	50	51	—	2.4
Total	636,608	666,925	684,639	667,022	643,886	100.0	−3.5

Source: Compiled from the *Transportation Statistics Monthly*, published by the Taiwan Ministry of Transportation, March 2010.

---

[18] Compiled from the *Hong Kong Logistics Transportation Industry Labor Survey Report* (2004–2008), published by the Vocational Training Programme for the Freight Logistics Sector, China.

Port is the largest international port in Taiwan and one of the important container ports in the world. Throughput at Kaohsiung Port in 2009 accounted for 52.1% of the total volume in Taiwan. Keelung Port is the import/export port and container port for high-value goods; Taichung Port is the port in central Taiwan for import/export cargo (containers), and the port of entry for energy, heavy industry and petrochemical raw materials; Hualien Port is responsible for the external transportation of eastern Taiwan. Currently, Taiwan has 18 civil airports, among which Taoyuan and Kaohsiung International Airports are two main airports to the outside world.

Currently, Taiwan has five free trade port zones including Keelung, Taipei, Taichung, Kaohsiung and Taoyuan Ports, with Suao Free Trade Zone to be added in January 2011. Since 2005 when the program of free trade ports was officially implemented, the total trade value increased from 1.2 billion NTD in 2005 to 143.47 billion NTD in 2009.

Taiwan's sea transportation consists of mainly international transportation, with international cargo throughput accounting for more than 80% of total cargo throughput. Total cargo throughput of Taiwan's sea transportation in 2009 was 248.71 million tons, 11.6% down compared with that in 2008, and the international cargo throughput decreased by 8.2%, as seen in Table 4.29. Container throughput of sea transportation was 11.71 million TEUs (of which cargo container made up 9.72 million TEUs), 9.8% down compared with that in 2008, as shown in Figure 4.9. Cargo throughput of Taiwan's air transportation in 2009 was 1,445,000 tons, down by 8.9% from that in 2008, falling for the fifth successive year. Cargo throughput of international air transport decreased by 9.9% compared with that in 2008.

The logistics industry of Taiwan features a large number of enterprises, but only a few large-scale international sea and air transportation companies. The majority of the enterprises are small-scale, serving mostly the local logistics market and mainly providing singular or dual services including traditional customs clearance, forwarding and storage. The number of logistics enterprises in Taiwan

Table 4.29   Cargo Throughput of Taiwan's Sea Transport for 2005–2009

	Total Throughput		International		Regional	
Year	Cargo Throughput (Million Tons)	Annual Growth Rate (%)	Cargo Throughput (Million Tons)	Annual Growth Rate (%)	Cargo Throughput (Million Tons)	Annual Growth Rate (%)
2005	280.62	−3.8	225.15	−4.5	55.47	−0.7
2006	274.23	−2.3	220.63	−2.0	53.60	−3.4
2007	292.34	6.6	242.70	10.0	49.64	−7.4
2008	281.26	−3.8	235.01	−3.2	46.25	−6.8
2009	248.71	−11.6	215.76	−8.2	32.95	−28.8

Source: Compiled from the *Transportation Statistics Monthly*, published by the Taiwan Ministry of Transportation, March 2010.

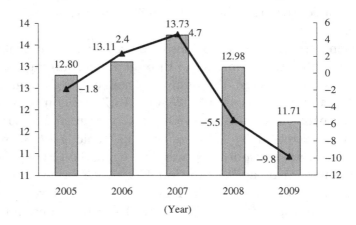

Figure 4.9   Container Throughput and Growth Rate of Taiwan for 2005–2009

Source: Compiled from the *Transportation Statistics Monthly*, published by the Taiwan Ministry of Transportation, March 2010.

in 2008 was 11,074 and the number of employees reached 199,000. Most of the logistics enterprises are trucking companies, numbering 4,933 and accounting for 44.5% of the total number. The business income of logistics enterprises was 706.33 billion NTD, of which the income of the sea transportation service industry was the highest with 297.58 billion NTD, accounting for 42.1% of the total revenue.

4.5.3 Policies and Measures for Logistics Development in Hong Kong and Taiwan

CEPA supplement VI and development plan for the logistics industry

In order to establish the hub connecting Mainland China with the global market, Hong Kong and the Mainland signed the *Closer Economic Partnership Arrangement* (CEPA) in 2003. To support Hong Kong in countering the financial crisis, CEPA Supplement VI was signed in May 2009 and implemented on October 1, 2009. CEPA Supplement VI stipulates that China will further open its market to Hong Kong in 20 service industries. Among these opened service fields, six are related to logistics services, i.e., comprehensive service, freight forwarding service, storage service, transportation service, distribution and railway transportation.

In Taiwan, the *Service Industry Development Plan* (2009–2012), issued in July 2009, listed the logistics service industry as one of the seven key emerging service industries. The Commerce Department of Taiwan implemented the *Plan for Promoting Logistics Industry Development* (2008–2011) in 2009, and put forward the *Logistics and Supply Chain Management Development Plan* to upgrade the service of its logistics industry and enhance its global competitive advantage. In addition, the *Plan for International Logistics Services* is being actively planned and promoted, aiming to match the development of cross-strait direct flights and the ECFA Agreement[19] and to strengthen the competitiveness of logistics development in Taiwan and its connection with the supply chain in the Asia-Pacific region.

---

[19] ECFA is the abbreviation for the *Economic Cooperation Framework Agreement*, which was officially signed in June 2010.

Development of cross-strait direct flights

Since the implementation of direct shipping, direct flights and direct post between the Mainland and Taiwan in December 2008, cross-strait cargo transportation and container throughput in 2009 was 57.8 million tons and 1.4 million TEUs, which respectively increased by 2% and 11% from that in the previous year. By the end of 2009, 71 of the 81 airports had launched direct flights, and 31 cities in the Mainland were opened to direct flights to Taiwan. Table 4.30 shows a list of important events relating to cross-strait direct flights.

Table 4.30　Important Events Relating to Cross-Strait Direct Flights in 2009

Date	Events
April 26, 2009	*Cross-Strait Air Transport Supplementary Agreement* and other two agreements were signed between the Mainland and Taiwan
May 16, 2009	The Ministry of Transportation issued nine policies and measures to further promote cross-strait direct shipping, including five newly added direct shipping ports or port areas (Tongling Port, Shidao Port, Laizhou Bay, Da Maiyu Port Area of Taizhou Port and Shen Jiamen Port Area of Ningbo-Zhoushan Port)
July 4, 2009	First anniversary of cross-strait charter flights and the opening of tourism for Mainland residents to Taiwan
August 31, 2009	Opening of scheduled flights between the Mainland and Taiwan
November 19, 2009	Opening of scheduled passenger liners between the Mainland and Taiwan
December 15, 2009	First anniversary of cross-strait direct shipping
December 28, 2009	The Ministry of Transportation announced three policies and measures for promoting cross-strait direct flights at the news conference marking the first anniversary of cross-strait direct shipping
December 30, 2009	Four Mainland cities (Taiyuan, Changchun, Nanning and Yantai) launched direct cross-strait scheduled passenger flights, increasing the number of Mainland cities with direct flights to Taiwan to 31

Logistics for the Chain Retail, Automobile and Petroleum Sectors

As the economy in China expanded in full force, various sectors grew in like proportion. Prominent among them are the chain retail, automobile and petroleum sectors; the logistics aspect of these three sectors has also been brought up to speed. This chapter expounds on the emergence, development, current status and the prospects for logistics in these three sectors. Each sector is also analyzed to highlight the existing logistics-related problems which could hinder the proper development of the sector.

5.1 Development of Chain Retail Logistics in China

5.1.1 *Overview of Chain Retail Logistics*

With the intensive reform of China's business and distribution systems in recent years, chain retail businesses developed rapidly. It has now basically replaced all kinds of traditional department stores that mainly operate under decentralized management. Chain retail is a common international business form for achieving standardization, specialization and integration of business activities by applying the principle of modern industrial mass production to businesses, so as to gain economies of scale. Logistics, which plays an important role in the operations of chain retail, has become one of the core competitive instruments for chain retail enterprises.

State of development of the chain retail industry in China

China's chain retail business began to appear in the early 1990s; it has taken the lead in the retail markets in large and medium-sized cities all over the country and demonstrated a rapidly expanding trend within the last decade. In 2008, due to the impact of the financial crisis, the number of chain retail customers and profit level decreased slightly, but the sales volume still increased by 20%, reaching 18.8% of the gross retail sales of consumer goods, while the number of stores maintained a growth rate of over 20%.

In view of the distribution of business types, the development of chain retail has expanded rapidly from supermarkets and convenience stores to other business formats, basically covering all aspects of business and service industries. Among them, the largest in number are chain supermarkets which mainly include the following: fresh grocery supermarkets, general merchandise supermarkets, comprehensive supermarkets, hypermarkets, theme-based shopping malls and convenience supermarkets. Next in scale are various chain specialty stores, ranging from household appliances, apparel and shoes to pharmaceuticals, automobiles, building materials, houses and other products. In China, three major high tides of consumption have been particularly prominent in recent years: consumers acquiring cars, families purchasing track housings, and the growing demand in the pharmaceutical market after the reform of the medical system. Driven by these factors, professional automobile chain stores, chain-type health pharmacies and chain-type real estate services have developed rapidly, championing a breakthrough development of the chain business in China. In some medium-sized and small cities, chain business formats also developed, from supermarkets and department stores to convenience stores, professional stores, specialty stores, large general supermarkets and home furnishing malls, thus further expanding their market shares.

Regarding the regional distribution, some sizable chain retail enterprises located on the eastern coast of China have started to exploit the markets in the Central and Western regions extensively. Their main approach is to set up branch companies and distribution centers, and to concentrate the development of chain stores in certain regions. These chain stores mainly take the form of supermarkets in order to facilitate the enterprises' gradual expansion into the surrounding and inland areas, and to reap additional benefits from the new markets. Cross-regional development of chain enterprises is a good start for deepening the development of the chain business in China.

Characteristics of chain retail logistics

Frequent change in commodity price and order

Usually, the price of fast-moving consumable commodities in chain supermarkets changes rapidly due to the fluctuation of demand and supply, as well as frequent promotions by the manufacturer or retailer. These factors can result in a high frequency of new product addition, elimination, exchange or disposal of dead stock. Meanwhile, a chain retail enterprise has many stores which generate a higher frequency of orders and often with time requirements; some small retail stores even demand deliveries twice a day.

Multiple processes in logistics operations

In addition to general processes such as transport and storage, chain retail logistics usually also includes many other operations such as bulk breaking, sorting, picking, labeling, returning and exchanging. Oftentimes they also need to handle some other problems such as gifts and returns of normal products and defects.

High diversity and degree of difficulty in logistics systems control

The chain retail logistics system entails a long and complex process, which not only increases the linkage costs of time and space during its operation, but also increases the difficulty in integrating systems control. After the bulk commodity purchase, chain retail enterprises have to distribute the goods to each branch store in a timely manner and in sufficient quantities. The distribution volume, distribution method, optimal distribution costs and delivery time are problems that must be considered by the logistics control center.

5.1.2 Development Status of Chain Retail Logistics

Rapid growth in scale of chain retail logistics

Since the early 1990s, chain retailing in China has grown rapidly both in size and in number; its dominant position in the retail markets improved continually, exhibiting a trend of rapid expansion. According to data published by the National Bureau of Statistics, by 2008, chain retail enterprises had opened up to 168,500 stores, with 1.97 million employees and a revenue of 2.05 trillion RMB, up 11.1%, 12.8% and 20.9% respectively compared with that in 2007 (Table 5.1).

In 2009, according to statistics published by China Chain Operations Association, the revenue of the top 100 retail enterprises (hereinafter referred to as the "top 100") was 1.36 trillion RMB, up 13.5% compared with that in 2008. This was the lowest growth rate since 1999, indicating that chain retail enterprises suffered a greater impact from the financial crisis than other industries. The total number of stores of the top 100 reached 137,000, increasing by 18.9%. The revenue of the top 100 accounted for 11% of the total retail volume of consumer goods, equaling the level in 2008. Among them,

Table 5.1   Overview of Chain Retail Enterprises

Index	Total Number of Stores (1,000)	Employees (Million Persons)	Total Value of Purchased Commodities (Billion RMB)	Total Size of Retail Area (Million m²)	Sales Amount (Trillion RMB)
2007	151.7	1.75	1,458.3	88.9	1.69
2008	168.5	1.97	1,719.3	102.0	2.05
Growth (%)	11.1	12.8	17.9	14.7	20.9

Source: Data from the website of the National Bureau of Statistics of China.
http://www.stats.gov.cn/tjsj/qtsj/lslssyqysj/2008/t20100129_402618136.htm.

Suning Electrical Appliances Group ranked No. 1 in the top 100, with a revenue of 117 billion RMB; GOME Electrical Appliances Group, Bailian Group Co., Ltd., Dashang Group Co., Ltd., and China Resources Vanguard Co., Ltd., ranked Nos. 2–5 with revenues of 106.8 billion RMB, 97.9 billion RMB, 70.5 billion RMB and 68 billion RMB, respectively. The revenue of the last enterprise included in the top 100 was 1.6 billion RMB, an increase of 10% compared to the last enterprise in 2008 with a revenue of 1.41 billion RMB.

Rapid increase in the proportion of consolidated delivery

After the transformation from the previous stage of the planned economy in China, many state-owned large-scale retail enterprises now possess a full range of logistics facilities and equipment. But due to the relatively laggard development of third-party logistics, the proportion of consolidated delivery in the industry has remained low. According to statistics published by the National Bureau of Statistics, for chain retail enterprises having 60 or more staff and a main business income of 5 million RMB or more, the proportion of consolidated delivery was only 42% in 2002. The low utilization of distribution facilities weakened the performance of consolidated purchasing and distribution, and seriously hampered the efficiency of chain retail enterprises. In recent years, with the change in status and management concepts of chain retail enterprises, as well as the rapid development of the third-party logistics industry, the proportion of consolidated delivery increased substantially in chain retail enterprises, reaching 78.8% in 2007 and 80.2% in 2008. However, considering the general status of a large number of small retail stores and rural retail businesses, the consolidated distribution rate of the whole industry is in fact still far below this level.

Dominance of enterprise-operated logistics distribution centers

In 2008, there were 3,604 distribution centers of chain retail enterprises in China; among them, 2,873 were self-owned, accounting for 80% of the total. In terms of the amount of commodity procurement, the ratio of self-owned to non-owned distribution centers was about

2.78:1. Currently, some large chain retail enterprises in China have set up their own logistics distribution centers for the main reason that a considerable number of them are established on the basis of traditional food companies, produce companies, grain stores and other networked facilities. All these traditional enterprises have ample venues, facilities and equipment, personnel, etc. But most of their logistics distribution centers have a low degree of informatization and mechanization, and mainly rely on manual operation, with low distribution efficiency and slow response to the stores.

In recent years, certain large enterprises have also built a number of logistics distribution centers with advanced technology. For instance, in 2002, Hualian Supermarket Co., Ltd. invested 80 million RMB to build the first modern chain distribution center in China, with an area of 20,000 m². This distribution center is equipped with high platforms and a large-span, single-floor building, which is capable of loading/unloading more than 80 trucks simultaneously at any one time; it has adopted a storage system with high-rise shelves and integrated bulk-breaking and picking operations. It introduced barcode technology, uses radio frequency (RF) mobile terminals and has fully implemented paperless logistics management with barcode technology in various operations, from receiving and confirming stock to warehousing until distribution. This center marked the beginning of implementing modern distribution technology in China's chain retail enterprises. After ten years of development, computer network information technology is now used widely. Therefore, the electronic tag selection system has spread rapidly, and radio frequency identification (RFID) and other technologies have been applied to the logistics distribution centers. For example, Taopu Distribution Center of the Agriculture, Industry and Commerce Supermarket Group was built in 2008, with an area of 90,000 m²; the center has fully adopted the RF and RFID technologies with the support of warehouse management systems (WMS).

Progress of supplier-owned and third-party logistics modes

Many large-scale manufacturing enterprises, including large appliance manufacturers (such as Haier, Hisense), food manufacturers (such as

Master Kong), as well as prominent foreign household chemical product manufacturers (such as Procter & Gamble) have set up their own sales distribution systems all over China, engaging their distribution channels directly with the distribution logistics activities of chain retail enterprises. The relationship between some large chain supermarket enterprises and these suppliers has changed from competition to cooperation, which not only reduces transaction costs, but also speeds up the transfer of supply and demand information between the demander and supplier. For example, Hualian Supermarket has established an automatic replenishment system with Shanghai Jieqiang Group and Procter & Gamble, changing from chain supermarket replenishment to supplier replenishment. This move enables enterprises to reduce the overall cost, inventory and the investment in tangible assets; it also benefits the consumers as they have more choices of higher quality and fresher food.

In recent years, with the increasing competitiveness of the logistics industry, some large retailers are gradually focusing on their main business, taking the path of professional development, while entrusting their own logistics distribution business to professional logistics distribution enterprises. This trend is more and more obvious as Beijing Wu-Mart, Yishang Group, Xidan Market and some other chain retail enterprises are actively exploring socialized logistics distribution services, engaging third-party logistics companies to provide them with centralized distribution centers, WMS as well as product distribution services.

Improved policy environment for chain logistics enterprises

In August 2005, China's State Council issued *Some Opinions of the State Council on Promoting the Development of the Circulation Industry*. The document indicates that the state will continue to promote the restructuring and reorganization of state-owned distribution enterprises, to speed up the cultivation of large distribution conglomerates, as well as to raise their competitiveness. This shows the important role and function of the distribution industry in the overall development of the national economy, and that the Government is paying more attention to its development.

China also issued a series of policies in supporting the development of chain logistics distribution centers. These policies include the following: (1) treating the construction of logistics distribution centers as a priority project and giving Treasury bond discount loans; (2) offering more conveniences in urban thoroughfare and parking to registered delivery vehicles of chain retail enterprises; (3) providing the necessary support to the companies developing chain retail and logistics distribution; (4) especially supporting profitable enterprises, widening their financing channels, helping them to raise social capital by increasing investment or stock shares, so as to expand the scale of business; (5) encouraging, through multiple modes such as asset reorganization and funds transfer, productive enterprises to reallocate their idle plants and equipment, as well as encouraging wholesaling and storage enterprises to reallocate their storage facilities and develop commodity distribution centers.

5.1.3 *Problems Existing in Chain Retail Logistics*

Low consolidated procurement and distribution
in small and medium-sized enterprises

The advantage of chain retail business lies in consolidated procurement and distribution which significantly reduces costs and enhances competitiveness. With the traditional distribution mode, the chain stores rely on two channels for procurement: the supplier and distribution center. Hence, the chain retail enterprise not only fails to realize consolidated delivery, but also suffers from hidden bloated purchasing costs due to low distribution efficiency. This traditional distribution mode may have little impact on some small chain retail enterprises; but when enterprises grow to a certain scale, especially when the scope of chain retailing becomes larger, this disparate mode will be fatal to the management and distribution of the chain retail enterprises. Therefore, the traditional distribution mode needs to be changed in order to realize consolidated distribution. This requires the presence of a distribution center, to create a unified sorting process for a variety of commodities in order to realize unified collective distribution. From an analysis of the characteristics of chain retail enterprises, suppliers and third-party logistics enterprises, it is clear that all three parties have a need for consolidated distribution to improve their efficiency.

Most medium-sized and small chain retail enterprises in China still practise traditional single-store procurement, thus losing the competitive advantage in retail price. The rate of consolidated distribution of these enterprises is also low, resulting in low vehicle loading rates and a high number of empty loads on return trips. Since each store delivers goods separately using sub-optimal routes, the cost of transport rises and the urban traffic jam worsens. In addition, due to the chain retail enterprises' limited investment in warehouses, vehicles as well as loading/unloading facilities, logistics operations still mainly rely on manual work, thus lacking efficiency.

Generally speaking, the chain retail enterprises in China have a high level of inventory, inefficient logistics operations and high logistics operating costs at present.

Further improvement needed in cooperation mechanisms with suppliers

The relationship between retail enterprises and suppliers needs further adjustment in China, and effective cooperation mechanisms need to be improved as well.

First, China's retail enterprises are often overly concerned with maximizing their own interests unilaterally, neglecting profit- and risk-sharing and seeking a win-win strategic cooperation relationship with their suppliers. In order to earn a profit, the retailer will wring the profit margin of the upstream suppliers: on one hand, depressing the purchase price; on the other hand, charging the suppliers numerous incidental expenses, even resorting to illegitimate approaches of delaying payment to the supplier and tying up its cash flow. The coordination mechanism for a win-win collaboration requires further improvement, and the concept of supply chain management still needs to be further expanded and implemented.

Second, due to many reasons such as inadequate laws and regulations and feeble market supervision, there exist some credibility problems between retailers and suppliers in China. Some retailers use their dominant position at the end of the sales channel to jeopardize the legitimate interests of suppliers in the transaction process. In recent years, there were numerous litigations between suppliers and retailers due to payment problems; many famous large supermarkets have been sued by suppliers because of delayed payment. Fewer than 50% of the large supermarkets in Guangzhou and other medium-sized and large cities can pay their suppliers on time. Some individual retail businesses after swindling bank loans and payments from providers, under the pretense of chain operation, immediately absconded with the money or closed down the business, claiming mismanagement. The conflict of capital flow has spread to the logistics distribution sector because many logistics enterprises are responsible for the function of collecting payment for goods, which also results in an increased risk in logistics. Meanwhile, the mistrustful relationship between suppliers and retailers heightens the difficulties of implementing joint distribution. In the last couple of years, with the promulgation of *The Code of Conduct for Fair Trading between Retailers and Suppliers*, this conflict has been reduced to some degree.

Low development level of distribution centers

Usually chain retail enterprises own logistics distribution centers specifically for distributing goods to stores. Some of the commodities are delivered directly from factories, thus reducing transport requirements. Some raw materials or semi-finished products provided by suppliers are processed, packaged, sorted and assembled in the logistics distribution center; this may increase the products' added value and reduce some other transport requirements. Yet logistics distribution centers in China still face many problems in management paradigms, management information system construction, investment in hardware, etc.

First, the management philosophy is lagging behind. Influenced by traditional concepts, the larger businesses tend to pay more attention to the effective control of the logistics process, often preferring self-operated logistics, expending resources to build their own complete system for purchasing, transport and storage, rather than utilizing an established distribution center. This is not only a waste of resources, but also stifles the development of logistics distribution centers.

Second, management information systems and hardware facilities are still backward. Currently, most chain retail businesses are limited in computer facilities and network applications, and lag behind in the construction of information systems. Thus the level of information sharing is low between the upstream and downstream in the retail supply chain. Meanwhile, due to the excessive investment in hardware facilities with long payback periods, most chain retail businesses adopt relatively inexpensive manual labor to carry out the logistics distribution operations. The backward information systems and hardware facilities have become obstacles to the development of chain retail logistics.

5.1.4 *Development Trend of Chain Retail Logistics in China*

Enhanced distribution functions for frozen and fresh food

First, the distribution centers of retail enterprises will increase or enhance the distribution functions for frozen and fresh food. With the competition heating up in the retail market and standards of living improving, consumers increase their demand for fast food, fresh semi-finished products and frozen food. Therefore, there is a trend in logistics and distribution for large-scale retail enterprises to set up food processing and distribution centers.

Second, food distribution centers which are predominantly of the wholesale type will appear. As powerful food wholesaling enterprises begin to assemble products and offer food distribution services specifically to independent supermarket stores, it will set the trend for specialty logistics distribution centers to be constructed in China. For instance, a distribution enterprise that specializes in meat, eggs, vegetables, milk, bread, ice cream and other fresh food logistics will form a multi-functional logistics center for logistics, room temperature storage, cold storage, packaging, circulation processing and delivery.

Trend of socialization of distribution

A socialized professional logistics service not only provides logistics services, but also handles the sales of commodities and management. The main purpose of a distribution service, besides obtaining service revenue, is to expand the scale of sales to increase the margin. On the basis of delivering goods, it keeps on strengthening its influence on medium-sized and small retailers, gradually developing a consolidated commodity delivery, merchandising and management service into a chain centralized management model, and finally forming a voluntary franchise chain network with different degrees of autonomy.

More intensive and widespread application of information technology

The information system of chain retail logistics includes the enterprises' internal management information system, the electronic data interchange (EDI) system or electronic ordering system (EOS). Since the late 1990s, the enterprises' internal management information system has matured so that chain retail enterprises can basically utilize their management information system to manage sales, purchasing and inventory. Some enterprises even adopt business analysis and intelligent management and supply chain management systems for sharing data with the suppliers, so as to improve efficiency. Also, with the popularization and promotion of e-commerce, retail enterprises, especially chain retail enterprises, have begun to apply online data transfer and ordering, using the Internet to share sales and inventory information with the logistics distribution centers and the upstream suppliers. They also provide cooperative support for the linking of online ordering, commodity inspection, returns, promotions, price changes, settlements and payments.

5.2 Status and Trend of the Development of China's Automotive Logistics

5.2.1 *Profile of Automotive Logistics*

Automotive logistics encompasses the comprehensive management activities aimed chiefly at automobiles, including transport, storage, packaging, safekeeping, hauling, reconfiguration and information services for automotive parts, accessories or whole vehicles, through all stages from production to sales.

Generally speaking, automotive logistics can be divided into parts and accessories logistics and vehicle logistics. Parts and accessories logistics refers to the logistics activities related to the supply, production and post-sales service of automotive parts and accessories needed for the assembly and production of vehicles. Vehicle logistics refers to the quick response and on-time delivery of vehicles in accordance with the delivery terms of the request, and quality guarantee of the client's order. Products involved in China's vehicle logistics include passenger cars, commercial cars, special vehicles and engineering vehicles, in multiple models and makes.

Basically China's vehicle logistics has gone through three phases[1] in its development:

Phase I covers the 30 years from the founding of the PRC in 1949 to the time China opened its doors to the world in 1979. During this period, the main purpose of China's automotive industry was to meet the demands of production in all trades. As one of the most important productive factors, automobile purchasing and distribution were planned by the state. The chief mode of "vehicle logistics" during this time was for the purchasing entity to designate a driver to pick up the vehicle at the production site.

During Phase II, from 1980 to 1990, vehicle sales was under a planned allotment system; the chief mode of logistics was for the purchaser to take possession of the vehicle from a distributor at his own expense. Independent proprietors that offered transport services to

---

[1] China Federation of Logistics and Purchasing, *China Logistics Key Projects Report* (2007), China Logistics Publishing House, Beijing, China, 2007.

vehicle purchasers were the chief providers of domestic vehicle logistics services in China.

Phase III saw the start of the modern period of automotive logistics. In 1990, Tianjin Anda Group developed the first professional truck to transport vehicles in China's automotive trade. This was known as "0 km delivery", as it delivered the vehicle to the buyer's designated destination. This marked the start of the new era of the automotive industry. With growing standards of living and changing concepts of automotive consumption, "0 km delivery" has become a basic requirement in the automotive trade. The mode of vehicle logistics also changed from truck-only to the present modes — chiefly highway transport supplemented by railway and waterway.

The development of automotive logistics works mainly in three aspects:

First of all, it effectively supports the rapid development of China's automotive industry. The demand for automobiles in China grew swiftly; automobile sales, whether of domestic makes, imported cars or used cars, are all prospering. Automotive logistics is an indispensable and key activity to realize successful automotive trading from the supply origin to the demand destination, offering powerful support to the development of the automotive industry.

Second, it improves the environment for automotive consumption to meet customers' demand for quality service. With the gradual maturing of the automotive market, the consumption of automobiles has become a very important part of people's life in China. Furthermore, consumers have higher and higher demands in terms of details such as perfect appearance, on-time delivery and service satisfaction. Logistics thus plays a very significant role in meeting the demand in the consumer market, as well as effectively improving the environment for automotive consumption and satisfying the consumers' requirements in terms of customer service.

Third, it helps to cut down the cost of production and thus strengthens the automotive manufacturers' competitiveness. Due to the influence of many factors such as the increasingly intensive competition in the global automotive market, the diversification of customer demands and the unpredictability of market conditions, many automotive manufacturers have taken actions such as reducing the unit production cost, improving flexibility in production and increasing the customers' satisfaction level. The success of these strategic measures relies to some degree on the development of automotive logistics. Above all, reducing logistics costs to lower the unit cost of automobiles and thus gain an advantage over the competition is currently still the most important factor considered by most of China's automotive manufacturers.

5.2.2 Development Status of China's Automotive Logistics

With the rapid development of China's national economy, the market environment for the development of automotive logistics also keeps improving. In 2009, the domestic demand for vehicles as well as parts and accessories increased rapidly in China, but the demand for international logistics dropped significantly due to the impact of the global financial crisis. These two different market conditions have shaped the development of automotive logistics from two different angles.

General increase in demand for automotive logistics

First of all, the output and sales volume of vehicles maintained a rapidly increasing pace in recent years. Table 5.2 shows the output and sales volume of vehicles in China. In 2009, the Government issued a series of policies to encourage automotive consumption, which further motivated the production of automobiles. The output and sales volume of passenger vehicles exceeded 10 million; the total output of cargo vehicles and passenger vehicles exceeded 13.6 million, ranking No. 1 in the world. Many professional automotive logistics enterprises saw an explosive growth in business in 2009. For instance, Anji-TNT Automotive Logistics Co., Ltd. realized a total shipment of 3 million vehicles, 30% up compared to the previous period. Beijing Changjiu Logistics Co., Ltd. also saw their business grow by 70%, as total shipment reached 0.9 million vehicles.[2]

---

[2] China Federation of Logistics and Purchasing, *China Logistics Development Report* (2008–2009), China Logistics Publishing House, Beijing, China, 2009.

Table 5.2 Output, Sales Volume and Growth of Vehicles in China for 2005–2009

Year	Output (Millions)	Growth of Output	Sales Volume (Millions)	Growth of Sales Volume
2005	5.71	12.56	5.76	13.54
2006	7.28	27.00	7.22	25.00
2007	8.88	22.02	8.79	21.84
2008	9.35	5.21	9.38	6.70
2009	13.79	48.00	13.64	46.00

Source: Data from the automotive statistics website of the China Association of Automobile Manufacturers.
http://www.auto-stats.org.cn/.

Second, the market scale of automotive parts and accessories kept increasing, with the trend of industrial clusters developing, and the demand for automotive parts and accessories logistics has also experienced a robust increase. Presently, there are 117 automotive manufacturers and more than 5,000 manufacturers of automotive parts and accessories. In 2007, the gross output value of China's automotive parts and accessories industry reached 670 billion RMB, and the value of sales reached 650 billion RMB. The export volume also increased quickly; some China-made brands started to enter international procurement systems. Along with the massive increase in automotive supply and demand in the domestic market, some six industrial clusters of automotive parts and accessories manufacturers have formed in China, i.e., in Northeast China, Beijing-Tianjin, Central China, Southwest China, the Yangtze River Delta and the Pearl River Delta.

Third, the imports and exports of automobiles declined markedly, interrupting the rising trend up till 2008. During 2005–2008, the total value of China's automotive imports increased from 15.314 billion USD to 33.107 billion USD, while the total value of China's automotive exports increased from 19.714 billion USD to 36.812 billion USD; both imports and exports kept growing at above 20% yearly. In 2009, due to the impact of the global financial crisis, the total value of China's automotive imports and exports dropped abruptly, down 13.85% compared with that in 2008, as shown in Table 5.3. The great

Table 5.3 Import and Export of China's Automotive Products for 2005–2009

Year	Total Value of Imports (Billion USD)	Total Value of Exports (Billion USD)	Total Value of Imports and Exports (Billion USD)	Growth of Imports and Exports (%)
2005	15.314	19.714	35.028	26.04
2006	20.870	28.144	49.014	39.93
2007	25.983	40.896	66.879	36.45
2008	31.429	49.729	81.158	21.35
2009	33.107	36.812	69.919	−13.85

shrinkage of automotive imports and exports in 2009 also decreased the demand for international logistics services for automotive products in China.

Acceleration of infrastructure construction for automotive logistics

Location of automotive logistics bases

Presently, there are six automotive logistics bases located in Changchun, Beijing-Tianjin, Wuhan, Shanghai, Guangzhou and Chongqing. Four coastal seaports, i.e., Dalian, Tianjin, Shanghai and Guangzhou, have invested sizable funds in constructing their local automotive logistics markets. In 2009, China FAW Group Corp. invested 860 million RMB in Chengdu city on projects of Chengdu Logistics Bases for Changchun Lujie Logistics Co., Ltd. and that of Import and Export Co., Ltd., China FAW Group Corp. The logistics bases will offer overall logistics services for Chengdu Branch, China FAW Group Corp. during the pre-production, mid-production and post-production stages. Geely Automobile Holdings Co., Ltd. plans to build three transit warehouses in Lanzhou, Jinan and Chengdu that will work as the logistics hubs for the transport of Geely's commercial vehicles. Beijing Changjiu Logistics Co., Ltd. has established a regional distribution center in Tianjin for domestic transshipment and delivery.[3]

---

[3] Meng Xi, "Research on the status and problems of China's automotive logistics", *Logistics Engineering and Management*, 2009(3): 1–4.

Multiple modes of transport for a green logistics system

Automotive logistics in China utilizes mainly three transport modes: highway (80%), rail (8%) and waterway (7%); the quantity of various transport tools is shown in Table 5.4. Recently, the proportion of transport by highway has started to decrease, while that by rail and waterway, which are more economical and safer, as well as multi-modal transport are rising. Take Anji-TNT Automotive Logistics Co., Ltd. for example. The company currently has more than 3,000 transport trucks, 348 box-cars, three river steamers, five seacrafts, two roll-on/roll-off docks and 33 warehouses. The company has cooperated with China Railway Special Cargo Services Co., Ltd., a subsidiary under the Ministry of Rail of the State Council, to establish two joint venture companies — Shanghai Andong and Shanghai Anbei — to engage in transport of vehicles by rail, establishing a rail transport platform covering all manufacturers and railway stations. In water transport, Anji-TNT Automotive Logistics Co., Ltd. has proceeded to construct the Shanghai Waigaoqiao Haitong Wharf, to establish a comprehensive water transport hub, forming a logistics center for integrating roll-on/roll-off docks, vehicle storage, parts and accessories delivery, etc. The composite utilization of multiple transport modes is helpful in cutting down logistics costs, reducing carbon emissions in logistics operations, and building a

Table 5.4   Various Transport Tools Related to China's Automotive Logistics

Transport Tool	Quantity	Load Per Unit (Vehicles)
Wheelbarrow	>6,000	6–8
Rail: Container	3,000	3–8
Rail: Specific car	500	10
Rail: Reformed car	500	6–8
Rail: Private car	578	8–12
Roll-on/roll-off ship	>10	100–400

Source: Zhang Xiaodong, "Review and prospect of China's passenger vehicle logistics, 2006", *Proceedings of 2007 China Logistics Development Report Meeting & 13th China Logistics Experts Forum*, January 2007.

modern and greener logistics system that is more precise, effective and friendly to the environment.[4]

Rapid development of automotive logistics enterprises

First, professional third-party automotive logistics service providers have become the principal service providers in the vehicle logistics industry. Statistics show that except for certain uncounted small enterprises in some local areas, there are around 60 automotive logistics enterprises in China, of which 53 are third-party logistics enterprises. A pack of logistics enterprises of moderate scale, with advanced management experience and steady business clients, lead the way for China's automotive logistics market. Among them, Anji-TNT, Beijing Changjiu, Tianjin Anda, COSCO Logistics, CITIC Logistics, Changchun Lujie, West Shanghai Logistics, Luyou Logistics and Jiubei Logistics are the outstanding representatives in this industry.

Second, the automotive logistics enterprises have started to integrate transport resources. Optimizing logistics networks and integrating transport resources have become essential avenues for automotive logistics enterprises to cut costs and improve work efficiency. Many enterprises have begun mutual cooperation and sharing of their network resources. Companies such as Beijing Changjiu, Anji-TNT, Cherry Logistics and Chang'an Mingsheng have established joint ventures to share their complementary advantages and resources, instituting the modern mode of collaborative transport. Henceforth, along with the automotive manufacturers' greater demand for lowering logistics costs and improving efficiency, integration of resources will be further developed through various means, thus forming a comprehensive win-win logistics platform.

Third, automotive manufacturers and logistic enterprises have molded a closer partnership than before. For example, SAIC Group and TNT Logistics Co. have established Anji-TNT Logistics Co.,

---

[4] China Federation of Logistics and Purchasing, *China Logistics Development Report* (2008–2009), China Logistics Publishing House, Beijing, China, 2009.

Ltd. by joint venture, and integrated all relevant logistics businesses into this new joint venture, making it the largest automotive logistics service supplier in China. Meanwhile, SAIC Group has realized the scientific management of its supply chain through Anji-TNT, improved its ability for quick response and cut its total logistics costs by more than 30%. COSCO Logistics has taken over the outsourcing business of Shanghai General Motors, resulting in the just-in-time (JIT) delivery of parts and accessories to the exact work stations, establishing a strategic partnership for mutual benefits. Beijing Changjiu Logistics is focusing on the linked actions of overall automotive logistics, integrating the customers' demands to propose and execute an automotive supply chain solution, and is also actively seeking international cooperation on inbound delivery of parts and accessories to manufacturers, global logistics, etc.[5]

5.2.3 *Problems Existing in China's Automotive Logistics*

High logistics costs due to scattered resources of transport capability

At present, due to the lack of a unified market entry system in China's automotive logistics industry, there exist problems of too many small-scale enterprises with poor competitiveness, as well as scattered resources and unreasonable allocation of transport capability.[6] First, most vehicle transport enterprises basically only deliver vehicles of their own brand, resulting in a very high (up to 37%) empty backhaul rate. Returning with empty loads causes problems like waste of energy and high transport costs. Second, currently most commercial vehicle logistics suppliers are relying on a single transport mode, and are unable to take advantage of multi-modal linked transport, resulting in high logistics costs.

---

[5] China Federation of Logistics and Purchasing, *China Logistics Development Report* (2006–2007), China Logistics Publishing House, Beijing, China, 2007.
[6] China Federation of Logistics and Purchasing, *China Logistics Key Projects Report* (2007), China Logistics Publishing House, Beijing, China, 2007.

Regulation of market competition

Under keen market competition, all automotive logistics enterprises more or less face problems of unregulated operations and vicious competition. First of all, excessive price competition in the industry has not only reduced the profit margin, but also led to problems of overloading, damaging of goods and low customer service quality. Second, lack of standardization for transport tools and non-uniform enforcement of regional policies make it difficult to ensure the safety of transport and logistics services. Third, business credibility needs improvement as problems such as delayed payment and insufficient transport capability exist with both the suppliers and the purchasers in fulfilling their contract.

Integrated and value-added features of logistics services

First, the services offered by most passenger vehicle logistics enterprises in China are only focusing on the transportation process. Even though some leading enterprises have achieved focused delivery service, they still have not realized a comprehensive logistics service which integrates transport, storage, delivery, information services, etc. Moreover, they are still lacking in services commonly provided by foreign enterprises such as vehicle cleaning, painting and waxing, customized installation and used vehicle logistics. Second, the application of IT technologies such as JIT, EDI, GPS, RFID in automotive logistics is still at the start-up stage, and the potential of modern logistics IT technology still needs further exploration. Therefore, there is ample room for the development of integrated and value-added automotive logistics services in China.

5.2.4 Development Trend of China's Automobile Logistics

Rapid expansion of demand in the automotive logistics market

In the period of the 12th Five-Year Plan (2011–2015), China's macro economy is expected to keep growing at a high speed, so the automotive industry is expected to develop quickly as well. As predicted by

China Association of Automobile Manufacturers, both the output and sales volume of automobiles in China will exceed 15 million vehicles in 2010.[7] This will surely bring a huge demand for automotive transport and logistics services, including that for passenger vehicles in China.

Further improvement of integrated automotive
transport system

At present, 85% of the vehicle logistics flow in China is concentrated on highways, while the transport capabilities in rail and waterway are not properly developed and utilized. With energy prices rising continually, the choice of more economical logistics equipment will be a key trend. Henceforth, China's logistics will gradually change from relying on highway transport to employing multi-modal linked transport.[8] By optimizing the rail and waterway transport capabilities and integrating highway resources, and by utilizing multi-modal shipping and inter-business collaboration, the backhaul loading ratio could be improved and the logistics operations cost for automobile manufacturers and automotive logistics enterprises would be reduced.

Bright prospects for integrated logistics and value-added services

As automotive manufacturers are expanding their production capacity and more new international enterprises are entering China's domestic automotive market, keener competition can be expected. Consequently, automotive manufacturers will place higher demands in terms of customer service, on-time delivery, safety, etc., on the logistics supplier. Hence, there exists a bright future for the development of integrated logistics and value-added services.

---

[7] "Output and sales of automobiles in good shape in Jan–May 2010", Ministry of Industry and Information Technology of the People's Republic of China, June 9, 2010. http://www.miit.gov.cn/n11293472/n11293832/n11294132/n12858417/n12858612/13259153.html.

[8] Zhang Xiaodong, "Review and prospect of China's passenger vehicle logistics, 2006", *Proceedings of the 2007 China Logistics Development Report Meeting & 13th China Logistics Experts Forum*, January 2007.

Standardization of automotive logistics

Standardization is the foundation for the development of modern logistics and a key method to improve its efficiency. Recently, China has issued several regulations pertaining to automotive logistics, namely, the *Transport Service of Passenger Vehicle Services Rules*, the *Transport Service of Commercial Vehicle Services Rules*, the *Storage Service of Passenger Vehicle Services Rules*, the *Transport Service by Water of Passenger Vehicle Services Rules* and the *Criteria for Judgment & Settlement for Damage Occurring in Passenger Vehicle Logistics*. Nevertheless, the level of standardization still requires further improvement. Pursuant to the *Specific Plan for the National Logistics Standardization, 2009–2011*, the Automotive Logistics Branch of China Logistics and Procurement Association is accelerating all relevant tasks on standardization for this industry. It also actively organizes the automotive logistics enterprises to promulgate the regulations through training, compiles the stipulations and cases to establish a platform for case research and on-site communication, as well as strengthen the establishment of standardization for automotive logistics enterprises.

5.3 Development of Petroleum Logistics in China

Petroleum is an important energy resource and a quality chemical raw material, and the petroleum industry is of vital importance to the national economy and the people's livelihood. In recent years, China's petroleum industry has developed rapidly due to the support of government policies, successive productivity upgrades of domestic enterprises, and the accelerated pace of international petroleum giants entering China's market. Presently, the petroleum logistics industry is facing unprecedented opportunities for development in China.

5.3.1 *Profile of Petroleum Logistics*

The petroleum industry and the special attributes of its product dictate a need for a professional and modern logistics system to ensure the development of a high-level petroleum industry. Such a logistics system not only reduces the logistics costs effectively, but also makes product transport safer and operations more professional. In general, petroleum logistics has its distinctive features in material forms, transport modes and operations requirements.

High safety and specificity requirements for facilities and equipment

Petroleum is flammable, explosive, prone to producing static electricity, and has certain toxic effects on the human body; consequently, it has high safety and specificity requirements for the facilities and equipment used in transport and storage. In China, the *Regulations on the Safety Administration of Dangerous Chemicals* stipulates that the enterprise engaging in the transport or storage of dangerous chemical goods must acquire certifications, its equipment and facilities must conform to national standards, and it must have a sound safety management system.

Advantages of pipeline transport for petroleum

In addition to highway, rail, air, water containers and large-tonnage petroleum tankers, the modes of transport for petroleum products include pipelines specialized for liquid and gas materials. Pipeline transport has some significant advantages such as low cost, large capacity, high security and good continuity, and is to some extent apt for replacing other traditional modes such as water or rail transport.

Large-scale transnational and transregional circulation

The distribution of petroleum resources is uneven and concentrated in certain regions worldwide. Quite often, a large distance exists between the origin of production and the consumption sites. The Middle East, Western Hemisphere, Eastern Europe, the former Soviet Union, Africa and Asia-Pacific are the main places of origin of crude petroleum, as shown in Table 5.5. However, global petroleum consumption is mainly concentrated in the developed and rapidly developing countries. The six countries with the highest petroleum consumption are the US, China, Japan, Russia, India and

Table 5.5   Distribution of Petroleum Output of Major Producing Regions in 2009

Crude Petroleum Regions	Petroleum Output (Billions Tons)	Proportion of Total World Output (%)
Middle East	1.055	29.9
Western Hemisphere	0.830	23.5
Eastern Europe and the former Soviet Union	0.641	18.2
Africa	0.434	12.3
Asia-Pacific	0.369	10.5
Western Europe	0.192	5.4
Total	3.521	99.8

Note: Major petroleum producers in (1) the Western Hemisphere are the United States, Canada, Mexico and Venezuela; (2) Eastern Europe and the former Soviet Union are Russia, Kazakhstan and Azerbaijan; (3) the Asia-Pacific regions are China, Indonesia, Malaysia and Australia; (4) Western Europe are Norway, the United Kingdom and Denmark.
Source: "World petroleum and gas reserves and production dynamics", China land resources network. http://www.clr.cn/front/read/read.asp?ID=188186; http://www.clr.cn/front/read/read.asp?ID=188846.

Germany, with the consumption accounting for about half of the global amount.[9] As a result, petroleum logistics forms a perpetual large-scale and cross-regional operation worldwide.

Huge stockpiles

Since the Organization of Petroleum Exporting Countries (OPEC) adopted the policies of reducing output and increasing price, major petroleum producers have suffered from domestic political turmoil. Since the demand for petroleum has expanded rapidly in recent years and crude petroleum prices in the international market fluctuated frequently, they have brought some negative effects to the economic growth of petroleum importing countries. Petroleum security has increasingly become the focus of attention around the world, leading

---

[9] Global rankings on petroleum consumption from CIA, website of China National Petroleum Corporation. http://news.cnpc.com.cn/system/2008/09/02/001198178.shtml.

to national petroleum strategic reserve systems being built worldwide, thus resulting in large volumes of strategic stockpiles.

5.3.2 *Current Status of China's Petroleum Logistics Development*

Crude petroleum suppliers and their geographical distribution

The total petroleum resources in China is about 100 billion tons, distributed mainly among the eight major basins in Bohai Bay, Songliao, Tarim, Ordos, Junggar, Pearl River Estuary, Qaidam and the East China Sea Shelf. The petroleum resources and the distribution of the major petroleum fields are shown in Figure 5.1.

The concentration of petroleum fields and the spread of consumption areas have led to the large-scale, transregional, long-distance petroleum transport in China. Presently, the average transport distance in China for cross-regional petroleum products is above 2,200 km. In addition, China's demand for imported crude petroleum is soaring;

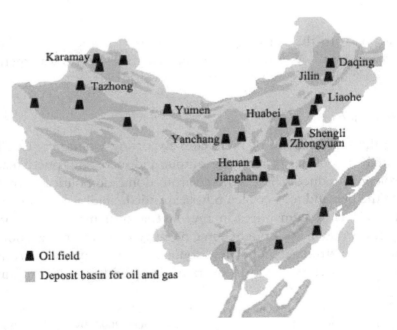

Figure 5.1   Distribution of Petroleum Resources and Main Petroleum Fields

Table 5.6 Major Countries Exporting Petroleum to China and Their Shares in 2009 (Top Six Countries)

Exporting Country	Region	Import Quantity (Million Tons)	Annual Growth (%)	Share (%)
Saudi Arabia	Middle East	41.86	15.09	20.54
Angola	Africa	32.17	7.62	15.79
Iran	Middle East	23.15	8.56	11.36
Russia	Central Asia	15.30	31.5	7.51
Sudan	Africa	12.19	16.11	5.98
Oman	Middle East	11.74	−19.5	5.76
Total	—	136.41	—	66.94

Source: Compiled from the Beijing Petroleum Market Management Information System website, Reuters Beijing website and the China General Administration of Customs website.

the major countries from which China imports petroleum and their shares in 2009 are shown in Table 5.6.

Currently, many of China's foreign petroleum cooperation projects resort to the arrangement of "petroleum share", meaning that China purchases shares or invests in petroleum construction projects in other countries, and takes a certain share of their petroleum output each year. In 2008, by participating in the exploration and development of foreign resources, PetroChina acquired a share of 30.5 million tons while Sinopec acquired 9 million tons.[10]

Gross national output and import/export of petroleum product

Because the main petroleum fields, Daqing and Shengli in the Eastern region, had reached their peak yields, because of typhoon damages to offshore petroleum facilities, and because of the impact of the international financial crisis, the gross national output of crude petroleum was 189 million tons in 2009, down 0.4% compared with that in 2008, as shown in Table 5.7.

---

[10] "From shortage of petroleum to exchange market shares with technology", *Republic Science & Technology Archives* 56. http://www.stdaily.com/kjrb/content/2009-09/29/content_110805.htm.

Table 5.7   Changes in Output of National Major Petroleum Products for 2006–2009

Product		2006 Total Output (Million Tons)	2006 Percentage Increase Over Previous Year (%)	2007 Total Output (Million Tons)	2007 Percentage Increase Over Previous Year (%)	2008 Total Output (Million Tons)	2008 Percentage Increase Over Previous Year (%)	2009 Total Output (Million Tons)	2009 Percentage Increase Over Previous Year (%)
Crude petroleum		184.00	1.7	186.32	1.3	189.73	1.8	189.00	-0.4
Product petroleum	Diesel	116.53	5.5	123.70	6.2	133.24	7.8	141.27	6.0
	Gasoline	55.91	3.7	59.94	7.2	63.48	5.9	71.95	13.3
	Kerosene	9.60	-2.9	11.53	20.1	11.65	1.0	14.79	27.0
	Total	182.04	4.3	195.17	7.2	208.37	6.8	228.01	9.4

Source: Compiled from the *National Economic and Social Development Statistical Bulletin* (2006–2009), China Petroleum and Chemical Industry Statistics Advisory Network, the *China Statistical Yearbook* (2009) and the National Statistics Bureau website.

Table 5.8   Import and Export of National Major Petroleum Products for 2008–2009 (Unit: Million Tons)

Product	Imports			Exports			Trade Balance (Imports — Exports)		
	2008	2009	Increase (%)	2008	2009	Increase (%)	2008	2009	Increase (%)
Crude petroleum	178.88	203.79	13.9	4.24	5.07	19.7	174.64	198.72	13.8
Product petroleum	38.85	36.96	−5.4	17.03	25.04	46.3	21.82	11.92	−45.4

Source: Compiled from the *China Statistical Yearbook* (2009), published by the National Bureau of Statistics of China, and from the General Administration of Customs website.

The increased demand and decreased output of petroleum further widened the gap between China's petroleum imports and exports. In 2009, its net import of crude petroleum was 199 million tons, up 13.8% compared with that in 2008, as shown in Table 5.8. Meanwhile, as the dependence on foreign petroleum trade increased, China's crude petroleum external dependency was up to 51.3%, which surpassed the warning line of 50% for the first time. Large-scale imports and exports of petroleum products drove up the demand for cross-border logistics services, consequently creating opportunities for international petroleum pipeline transport services and ocean petroleum tanker transport services.

Petroleum product manufacturers, market structure and geographical distribution

At present, a diversification pattern has formed in the domestic petroleum products market, and the competition among the state-owned, private- and foreign enterprises has become fiercer. Among them, the representatives of large state-owned enterprises — Sinopec and PetroChina — hold dominant positions.

In 2009, Sinopec, as the industry's key enterprise, made progress in its production management. Its annual crude petroleum output totaled 42.42 million tons, up 1.48% compared with that in 2008; the output of product petroleum (gasoline, diesel, kerosene) was 113.68 million tons, up 5.87% compared with that in 2008, as shown in Table 5.9.

In 2009, PetroChina produced 103.13 million tons of crude petroleum, down 4.73% compared with that in 2008; the output of product petroleum (gasoline, diesel and kerosene) was 80.45 million tons, up 1.55% compared with that in 2008, as shown in Table 5.10.

Table 5.9 Sinopec's Production of Crude Petroleum and Product Petroleum for 2008–2009

Item	Unit	2008	2009	Rate of Changes (%)
Crude petroleum output	Million tons	41.80	42.42	1.48
Processing quantity of crude petroleum	Million tons	171.14	182.62	6.71
Product petroleum output	Million tons	107.38	113.68	5.87
Gasoline	Million tons	29.65	34.43	16.12
Diesel	Million tons	69.74	68.86	−1.26
Kerosene	Million tons	7.99	10.39	30.04

Source: Compiled from data published on the Sinopec website.

Table 5.10 PetroChina's Production of Crude Petroleum and Product Petroleum for 2008–2009

Item	Unit	2008	2009	Rate of Change (%)
Crude petroleum output	Million tons	108.25	103.13	−4.73
Processing quantity of crude petroleum	Million tons	125.30	125.12	−0.14
Product petroleum output	Million tons	79.22	80.45	1.55
Gasoline	Million tons	25.46	25.82	1.41
Diesel	Million tons	50.16	50.99	1.65
Kerosene	Million tons	3.60	3.64	1.11

Source: Compiled from data published on the PetroChina website.

Table 5.11   Regional Distribution of Top 100 Manufacturing Enterprises in Crude Petroleum Processing and Petroleum Products

Region	Number of Enterprises	Region	Number of Enterprises	Region	Number of Enterprises
Beijing	4	Fujian	2	Heilongjiang	3
Tianjin	5	Guangdong	10	Jilin	2
Hebei	2	Guangxi	4	Liaoning	12
Shanxi	1	Hubei	2	Shanghai	2
Inner Mongolia	1	Hunan	1	Jiangsu	10
Shandong	25	Sichuan	1	Zhejiang	4
Henan	2	Ningxia	2	Anhui	1
Shanxi	1	Xinjiang	3	Total	100

Source: Compiled from data published by the China Petroleum and Chemical Industry Advisory Statistics Network.

From the perspective of regional distribution, ranking the domestic crude petroleum processing and petroleum product manufacturing enterprises by their sales revenue, the top 100 enterprises are mainly distributed in the Bohai Rim Region, northeast region, Yangtze River Delta, Pearl River Delta and some western provinces such as Ningxia and Xinjiang, as shown in Table 5.11.

Product petroleum sales of distributors

The demand for domestic petroleum products has soared in recent years. In 2009, China consumed 38.8 billion tons of petroleum, up 7.1% from the previous year,[11] becoming the second-largest petroleum consumer in the world, after the US. Distributors of petroleum products include importers and domestic wholesalers and retailers; among them, the large state-owned enterprises Sinopec and PetroChina also hold dominant positions. In 2009, the total volume of domestic sales of product petroleum by Sinopec was 124.02 million tons, up 0.8% from the previous year, as shown in Table 5.12.

---

[11] *2009 China Statistical Bulletin of National Economic and Social Development*, National Bureau of Statistics of China, 2010.

Table 5.12   Product Petroleum Sales of Sinopec for 2008–2009

Item (Million Tons)	2008	2009	Rate of Change (%)
Total sales volume of domestic petroleum products	122.98	124.03	0.8
Retail volume	84.10	78.90	−6.2
Direct sales volume	19.63	25.61	30.5
Wholesale volume	19.25	19.52	1.4

Source: Compiled from data published on the Sinopec website.

Table 5.13   Product Petroleum Sales of PetroChina for 2008–2009

Name of Item	2008	2009	Rate of Change (%)
Total sales volume of product petroleum (million tons)	82.93	88.75	7.0
Number of gas stations	17,456	17,262	−1.11

Source: Compiled from data published on the China National Petroleum Corporation website.

In 2009, the total volume of domestic sales of product petroleum by PetroChina was 88.75 million tons, up 7.0% from the previous year, as shown in Table 5.13.

Petroleum logistics entities and management mode

China's petroleum logistics grew with the development of the petroleum industry, and currently has three co-existing forms: state-owned, private- and foreign-invested enterprises; private-owned and third-party modes of business also co-exist in the market.

China's state-owned petroleum logistics business entities can be divided into three categories according to business type. The first type is self-operated by petrochemical production or trading enterprises, mainly Sinopec, PetroChina and other large state-owned enterprises; each one forms its own logistics system due to production or trade needs. The second type is where integrated third-party logistics companies have been extended to the petroleum industries. The third type consists of professional logistics services companies based at petrochemical parks and petrochemical bases.[12]

The rise of the domestic private economy also led many private enterprises to begin engaging in petroleum products logistics business. Private petroleum logistics business entities are mainly self-operated logistics divisions of private petrochemical enterprises such as Taishan Petrochemistry and Baota Petrochemistry, which have built their own professional logistics systems. Among the third-party logistics companies, relatively few provide petroleum logistics services, and their service functions, quality and efficiency still remain to be improved.

The upward development of the domestic petroleum industry and the full liberalization of the petroleum logistics fields have also accelerated the entry of international petrochemical logistics giants such as Vopak of the Netherlands, Oiltanking and Suttons. Most of them set foot in the Chinese market by resorting to joint investment and cooperation with domestic logistics storage and transport enterprises. In addition, the opening-up policy also allowed some major foreign shipping companies access to inland water transport for domestic petroleum and chemical products.

Profile of petroleum pipeline transportation

At the present time in China, the majority of land transport of crude petroleum is through pipelines. Meanwhile, the strategic channels of natural gas are also gradually being established, going in all directions and connecting land and ocean. Since the founding of the PRC, its level of petroleum and gas pipeline transport has increased steadily. With the acceleration of production in the Tarim, Turpan-Hami, Junggar, Qaidam, Ordos and Sichuan Basin petroleum and gas fields, and the increase in imports of foreign petroleum and gas, pipeline construction in China has entered a

---

[12] "Status of petrochemical logistics development and the options for China's enterprises", *Chemical On-Line*, September 8, 2006.

climatic period of rapid development. During 1995–2008, the total mileage of China's petroleum and gas pipelines increased about 4,000 km annually.[13]

Since 1996 the coverage of China's crude petroleum pipeline network has expanded continually. Presently the crude petroleum pipelines which have been completed and put into production are as follows: the Kushan Line (Korla-Shanshan), the Lunku Double Line (Lunnan-Korla), the Zhongyin Line (Zhongwei-Yinchuan), the Yonghuning Line (Ningbo-Shanghai-Nanjing), the Yonghang Line (Ningbo-Hangzhou), the Yichang Line (Yizheng-Changling), the Hazhong Line (Kazakhstan-Alashankou-Dushanzi), the Western Line (Urumqi-Lanzhou), the Caojin Line (Caofeidian-Tianjin) and the Jibai Line (Jiyuanyou-Baibao). Previously existing pipelines plus the newly added ones form a regional crude petroleum pipeline network with large areas throughout Northeast, North, South Central, East and Northwest China.

The scale of China's product petroleum pipeline transport increases annually as the number of new pipelines increases. The main and feeder pipelines that have been built include the following: Fushun-Bayuquan, Karamay-Urumqi, Tianjin Port-Capital International Airport, Zhenhai-Hangzhou, Zhenhai-Caojing, Jinshan-Minhang, Gaoqiao-Jinshan, Jingmen-Jingzhou, Lanzhou-Chengdu-Chongqing, Lanzhou-Zhengzhou-Changsha, Luoyang-Zhengzhou-Zhumadian, Shijiazhuang-Taiyuan, Dagang-Zaozhuang and Maoming-Kunming. Currently, the regions of Northeast, Northwest, East and North China have formed a regional pipeline network for product petroleum; the northwest, southwest and Pearl River Delta regions have built the main product petroleum pipelines. The pipeline transport framework of transporting petroleum from the north to the south, and from the west to the east is taking shape.

With the founding of the China-Kazakhstan petroleum pipeline, China has begun to import petroleum and gas by pipeline. Strategic China-Russia and China-Myanmar petroleum and gas pipelines will

---

[13] Qi Aihua, "Chinese oil and gas pipeline transport development status and analysis of associated problems", *International Petroleum Economics*, 2009(12): 57–59.

be built in 2010–2015. By then, the three main land import channels of the northwest, the northeast and the southwest will be basically framed; together with maritime transport routes, they will constitute the four main channels of the diversified structure of China's petroleum and gas imports.

By 2009, China had built 17,000 km of crude petroleum pipelines and 14,000 km product petroleum pipelines, forming a primary cross-regional petroleum and gas pipeline network. With the increase in pipeline mileage, pipeline transport is playing an even more prominent role in China's petroleum transport system.

Policy environment for the development of petroleum logistics

The national strategic plans have put forward new requirements on the petroleum industry and created new opportunities for it. In December 2008, the State Council approved the *National Plan for Mineral Resources (2008–2015)*. This plan stipulates that six new petroleum fields with a reserve of a hundred million tons will be explored by 2010, with crude outputs up to 190 million tons or more; during 2011–2015, about ten new petroleum fields with a reserve of a hundred million tons are expected to be discovered, with petroleum outputs up to 200 million tons or more by 2015. In May 2009, the State Council promulgated the *Plan on Adjusting and Revitalizing the Petrochemical Industry*, specifying that by 2011, China's crude petroleum processing capacity would reach 405 million tons; the volume of petroleum products would reach 247.5 million tons; the industry structure would become rational, the practice of transporting product petroleum from the south to the north would have been improved; and that China would have accelerated the construction of reserve facilities and seized the opportunity to increase the national petroleum reserves.

The legislation related to the management and logistics operation of the petroleum industry has been gradually improved. First, laws and regulations are becoming sounder, aiming at safety in production. Second, the state has begun a concerted effort to curb the negative effects on the environment from the production and operation of those high-risk and high-pollution industries. This will inevitably have a greater impact on the management of the petroleum industry and its logistics operations.

The Chinese Government's strategy of energy diplomacy has proceeded in an all-around way. In recent years, China has signed various forms of documents on energy cooperation with Canada, Peru, Russia, Australia and Myanmar. For example, in March 2009, China and Myanmar signed the *Government Agreements on the Construction of Petroleum and Gas Pipelines between China and Myanmar.*

The trade of product petroleum has been fully deregulated. According to the commitments to the international community when joining the WTO, China opened its retail markets of product petroleum in December 2004, and then opened the petroleum wholesale business further in December 2006, realizing full liberalization of the domestic product petroleum trade.

5.3.3 *Problems Existing in Petroleum Logistics in China*

Safety of petroleum logistics

The latent safety risks of China's petroleum logistics lie mainly in three aspects. First, the safety management of petroleum logistics operators is inadequate. Second, the government agency's management of petroleum logistics still needs to be strengthened. Third, the specificity of petroleum logistics equipment needs to be improved. For example, most vehicles for transporting petroleum products in developed countries have installed the global positioning system (GPS). However, in China, although the state has instituted relevant regulations and requirements, relatively few such transport vehicles have installed the system owing to limited funds.[14]

---

[14] Chen Fangjian, "China's chemical logistics is developing", *Logistics Technology*, 2006(9): 107–108.

High cost of petroleum logistics system

The logistics cost of China's petroleum companies is over 100 billion RMB per year. The main reasons of the high cost of the petroleum logistics system are as follows. First, the logistics operations have not received adequate attention in the production and construction of petroleum fields; the investment in technological transformation and the level of management are low. Second, because of the wide business span, extensive coverage and frequent transactions of petroleum companies, the required variety of professional logistics facilities are distributed throughout the country, making it difficult to explore their scale advantage to the fullest.[15]

Facilities and technical conditions of petroleum logistics

First, on the whole, the supply of special wharfs for petroleum products and high-standard storage facilities are inadequate to meet the demand, and their rational layout also should be attended to.[16] Second, the construction of professional petroleum logistics bases and centers, mainly serving specific regions or cities, is lagging behind. Third, the information infrastructure and information technology applications are also lagging behind because of the limitations of manpower, material resources and technical conditions; the majority of petroleum logistics business entities have not yet adopted a comprehensive information management system.

Management of petroleum logistics enterprises

Domestic petroleum logistics business entities have obvious disadvantages in various aspects. First, the modern concept of logistics services has not been effectively ingrained in the strategic decisions,

---

[15] Li Binggang, "Building a modern logistics system in China's oil industry", *China Markets*, 2007(5): 50–51.
[16] Hou Jie, "Opportunity and challenge co-exist in China's chemical logistics", *China Chemical Industry News*, September 12, 2005.

daily business operations and management. Second, under the influence and restraint of a long-term planned economy, internal logistics resources lack integration, the utilization rate of facilities and equipment is still relatively low, and advantages from aggregate operations are not evident. Third, professional logistics talents are in short supply.

5.3.4 *Development Trend of China's Petroleum Logistics*

Port logistics in the construction of the petroleum logistics system

The status of port logistics will become more important in China's petroleum logistics system, and the development of petroleum logistics in the port areas will further improve the construction of China's overall logistics system. In 2008, about 90% of imported crude petroleum depended on ports for entry into China. According to statistics, at just 300,000-ton-level ports, there are about 20 blocks of petroleum terminals already completed, under construction or to be constructed; so port logistics is becoming an important link in the transport of crude petroleum.

Spatial structure of petroleum logistics due for change

With the further implementation of the strategies for "diversified" energy diplomacy, the traditional spatial structure of petroleum logistics is bound to transform. During the period of the 11th Five-Year Plan, due to the need for crude petroleum imports from Russia, Kazakhstan, the Middle East and Africa, together with marine imports and domestic crude petroleum production, China either expanded or newly built the corresponding petroleum pipelines,[17] such as the China-Myanmar petroleum and gas pipelines. Henceforth, China will build a coastal pipeline network, which will constitute a better regional

---

[17] "China-Myanmar petroleum and gas pipelines: Reinforcement of petroleum security", *China Economics Herald*, June 9, 2009. http://www.ceh.com.cn/ceh/jryw/2009/6/9/48036.shtml.

pipeline system for Western China, Central China, South Central China, Southwest China, Northeast China, the Bohai Rim Region, the Yangtze River Delta and the Pearl River Delta. This will speed up the construction of facilities for arterial pipelines, peak load adjustment and reserves, etc.[18]

Value-added services as the competitive hotspot
for petroleum logistics enterprises

Petroleum logistics include not only regular services such as transport, storage, loading and unloading, but also a series of value-added services such as designing logistics networks, providing solutions for supply chains, order management and information services. Similar to the experience of foreign logistics industries, the value-added services have extended in an all-around manner to the entire logistics industry, and become a mark of excellent logistics services. The value-added services of China's petroleum logistics will have a wide-open sphere in which to expand in the future.

Green logistics as the main guiding tenet for petroleum logistics

Although China has achieved rapid development in petroleum logistics in recent years, multiple accidents and the corresponding contamination thereof have received much attention in society for some time. Domestic legislation and regulations pertaining to production safety and environmental protection are being gradually improved, and the law enforcement is being intensified continually. Petroleum logistics management entities must pay more attention to the problems of production safety and environmental protection in the process of logistics operations; green petroleum logistics will be an important tenet in guiding their daily business activities.

---

[18] "Petroleum and gas networking is forming up in China", *China Energy News*, November 2, 2009.

CHAPTER 6

Logistics of Significant Events and Topics

Logistics is not only a process and a collection of coordinated activities linking many entities, or moving goods through sprawling networks, it has also become a vital function in people's daily lives. Besides the planned, cost-based and efficiency-oriented flows and activities, logistics functions also to provide critical and invaluable support for unplanned, urgent disaster relief situations or unique, grand-scale, special events.

This chapter presents two such recent incidents which occurred in China to illustrate emergency logistics and special event logistics. For emergency logistics, the recent cases of massive earthquakes in Wenchuan and Yushu of China are cited to discuss issues of disaster response organizations, reserves, mobilization, communication and command, action planning and execution. Post-disaster evaluation of emergency preparedness and lessons learned are also discussed.

The highly successful Beijing Olympic Games held in China in 2008 is used to illustrate the planning, coordination, organizational command and seamless orchestration of the logistics activities in support of this special world event. The numerous tasks requiring precise, secure and on-time deliveries could only be accomplished through well-planned, strictly executed logistics and the cooperation and expertise of participating agencies and enterprises.

Finally, the chapter concludes with a description of China's international trade logistics which has transformed and grown rapidly in recent years. The logistics capability of seaport and airport facilities and service providers are discussed in detail.

6.1 Emergency Logistics: Wenchuan and Yushu Earthquakes

6.1.1 *Profile of Emergency Logistics*

From 1998 onward, some supernatural and sudden disasters, e.g., floods, SARS, snowstorms and earthquakes, occurred one after another in China, creating devastating threats to the national economy, people's lives and safety. During the rescue operations after each disaster, emergency logistics played a significant role and has become of particular concern to the Government and society.

Emergency logistics entails the process of organizing, in an orderly way, the delivery of materials from the point of origin to needy destinations in order to cope with a public emergency; it is also a kind of special organized activity to ensure that the emergency demand for personnel or funds is met. Different from regular logistics which aims at maximum profit, emergency logistics seeks maximum efficiency within the shortest time period, thus meeting the urgent demand for logistics as a result of the public emergency.

Compared with regular logistics, emergency logistics has some distinguishing features. First, the most typical feature of emergency logistics is the suddenness of and the unpredictability following a public emergency incident. Second, the economic benefit sought in regular logistics will not be considered the main purpose in emergency logistics. Due to the need for timeliness, more expensive but faster transport tools may be adopted for emergency deliveries, or transport capabilities of other materials may be sacrificed to guarantee the delivery of materials for emergency relief. And finally, because emergency logistics always happens due to natural disasters, urgent public sanitary or safety incidents, it usually covers a wide scope and has a massive effect and influence on society. Hence, emergency logistics involves multiple directing entities and are carried out according to the principle of "mobilization of all the people, participation by the entire community, under the leadership of the Government", and if needed, even engaging the military forces according to the laws and regulations.

6.1.2 *Development Status of China's Emergency Logistics*

Organization of emergency logistics systems

The organization and command of China's emergency logistics are executed in an orderly manner within the existing system of emergency management, as shown in Figure 6.1. The State Council is the highest command in the structure of managing public emergency tasks. Under the leadership of the Premier, the Standing Committee and relevant emergency command authorities are responsible for all the management affairs in case of a public emergency event. Serving as the operational hub, the Emergency Response Office instituted under the General Office of the State Council is responsible for guard duties, information gathering and general coordination of diverse tasks. Meanwhile, the other departments of the State Council, e.g., the Ministry of Civil Affairs, the Ministry of Railways, the Ministry of Transport, the Ministry of Commerce and the Ministry of Public Health, will follow the relevant laws and regulations as well as perform their duties to draft and execute the specific or divisional solutions to cope with the public emergency in the relevant category and carry out the decisions made by the State Council.

Local governments at all levels, as the leaders in their regions for coping with emergency events, are responsible for all the management affairs in various emergency events occurring in the local area. By the end of 2007, all provincial and municipal as well as 92% of the county governments had established or assigned the governing authority for emergency response; all provincial, 96% of the municipal as well as 81% of the county governments had established or assigned the executing authority for emergency response.[1]

The State Council and local governments at all levels are responsible for establishing a database of various talents, consulting the relevant experts on what decisions to make upon the occurrence of an

---

[1] Hua Jianmin, "Several problems in the jobs of China's emergency management", *People's Daily*, December 29, 2007.

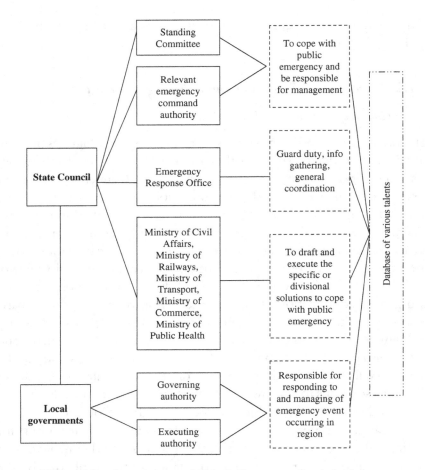

Figure 6.1   Organization of China's Emergency Logistics System

Source: Compiled from *Overall Contingency Plans for National Public Emergencies*, published by the State Council of China, 2005.

emergency. If necessary, these experts can also participate in the tasks of dealing with a public emergency.

Relevant laws and policies regarding emergency logistics

At present, China has not instituted specific laws for emergency logistics; rather, all relevant content is scattered across various emergency event-related laws and regulations. For example, laws and regulations, such as the *Law of the People's Republic of China on Donations for Public Welfare*, the *Interim Measures for the Administration of Donations for Disaster Relief*, the *Law of the People's Republic of China on Protecting Against and Mitigating Earthquake Disasters*, the *Flood Control Law of the People's Republic of China*, the *Regulation on the Urgent Handling of Public Health Emergencies*, all contain relevant content on emergency logistics. In January 2006, the State Council issued the *Overall Contingency Plans for National Public Emergencies*. In Chapter 4 of this Plan, "Emergency Assurance", the assurance of emergency logistics has been clarified. In November 2007, the *Emergency Response Law of the People's Republic of China* was put into effect; Article 32 of this Law specifically declares that "The State shall establish a complete system for the storage and assurance of emergency materials, and improve the system for governing the custody, production, storage, allocation and urgent delivery of significant emergency materials".

Reserve system for emergency materials

In China, materials for disaster relief are governed by multiple departments with the National Material Reserve for Disaster Relief as the center. Among them, the Department of Civil Affairs is responsible for the reserve of livelihood materials such as clothing and tents, while the Departments of Public Health, Transport, Foods are responsible for other emergency materials such as medicine, vehicles and food.

Pursuant to the assessed requirements for disaster relief after the earthquake in Zhangbei County[2] in 1998, the Ministry of Civil Affairs and the Ministry of Finance jointly issued *The Notice of Establishing a Reserve System of Central Disaster Relief Materials*, which required the Central Government and local governments,

---

[2] On January 10, 1998, a M6.2 earthquake occurred in Zhangbei County, Hebei Province, killing 49 people and causing direct economic loss of 2.4 billion RMB.

especially for regions with frequent natural disasters, to maintain reserves of certain emergency materials. After years of construction and reorganization, there are currently ten state-level emergency material reserve units established in the whole country (namely, the emergency material reserves of the Ministry of Civil Affairs). In addition, emergency storehouses are established in all provinces with a total acreage of 137,943 m² (including state-level emergency materials reserves) and a total capacity of 368,623 m², covering 157 cities and 447 counties.[3] Every year the Central Government appropriates 50 million RMB to maintain its reserve of emergency materials, mainly tents, clothing and quilts.

Furthermore, China has established a national medicine reserve system since the early 1970s; the Government has appropriated designated funds to build 13 medicine reserve storehouses in the country. By the mid-1990s, the total amount of medicine reserves was valued at 2 billion RMB. Since 1997, China has established a central-local dual-level medicine reserve system, in which local reserves are the principal ones and central reserves are supplementary, acting on a dynamic-reserve and compensatory-relocation mechanism. The basic operation mode is as follows: several large-scale state-owned pharmaceutical companies are designated as the national medicine reserve units; the Department of Public Health proposes a list of reserved medicines according to the assessed need for national disasters and epidemics; the Economic Planning Department issues the reserve plan; and the Finance Department appropriates the reserve funds for the designated companies upon approval. Then, as the national medicine reserve units, these companies would stock all emergency medicines on the list; a pre-specified proportion of these reserved medicines can be circulated in the market for the purpose of refreshing the stock held. In case of any outbreak of epidemic disease, they will supply the medicines to the disaster areas at the required time and in the required quantity.

---

[3] Gao Jianguo *et al.*, "The historical and present situation of the state reserve system of rescue goods and materials", *Recent Developments in World Seismology*, 2005(4).

Distribution of emergency materials

The distribution of emergency materials is under the command and control of the Department of Transport Administration. The tasks mainly involve acquiring and allocating the vehicles, utilizing all four transport modes (rail, highway, air and water), relying on the existing logistics parks, centers or distribution centers in the emergency area, and mobilizing logistics enterprises to transport and distribute emergency materials.

Concerning the dispatching of vehicles, there are two main sources of vehicles for delivering emergency materials: one is the military force; the other is commercial logistics companies under a long-term lease agreement to provide vehicles in case of a disaster event. Furthermore, in order to ensure the smooth delivery of emergency materials, a "Green Corridor" shall be opened in times of need. For example, in 2003, for delivering the materials for precautions against SARS, China lifted the limits on the transport capability of the delivery stations and project approval, allowing priority shipping and loading of these materials through a "Green Corridor". Under this system, the Liuzhou Railway Station finished the priority loading of all medicines in 13 minutes; the Harbin Railway department took only four hours to dispatch empty trains from 15 stations and dispatched 34 priority cargo trains to Beijing within only three days.

Management of emergency materials

Emergency materials in China are mainly from four sources, i.e., central reserve, state allocation, public donations and government procurement. Whenever a major natural disaster occurred, emergency materials gathered from all regions were of various kinds and in huge quantities. Therefore, to manage the emergency materials, China issued several laws and regulations to standardize the management, allocation and use of emergency materials, e.g., the *Law of the People's Republic of China on Donations for Public Welfare* (September 1999), the *Measures for the*

Administration of Central Disaster Relief Materials (December 2002) and the *Measures for the Administration of Donations for Disaster Relief* (October 2007).

Informatization of emergency logistics

The informatization system of China's emergency logistics is established through integration of the application systems of both the Government and relevant institutes and enterprises by merging the existing emergency logistics informatization systems. At present, an information platform for emergency logistics management has been established, linking the Central Government and local governments, relevant institutes, organizations, as well as combining military logistics and regional logistics. The platform can show comprehensive geographical information, resource allocations, logistics channels, emergency forces, etc. In addition, the Government has also strengthened the construction of an emergency logistics database, actively urged emergency logistics enterprises to link their terminal nodes to its emergency response network, realizing the linkage and sharing of emergency information resources on the governmental network.

During the massive snowstorm that occurred in South China and the May 12 Wenchuan earthquake in Sichuan Province in 2008, satellite navigation was widely applied in logistics management. The implementation realized the 24-hour delivery of oil and gas to disaster areas, seamless coverage of telecommunication, command and logistics management, playing a critical role in ensuring the supply of oil and other materials. According to statistics, there were in total 15 satellites (consisting of nine different models) serving after the May 12 Wenchuan earthquake to offer assistance in disaster relief, including the "Clouds" series meteorological satellite, the "Resources" series earth observation satellite, the "Compass" navigation satellite, the "Remote Sensing" series satellite and the "Beijing No. 1" small satellite. The modern equipment has greatly improved the construction of informatization for emergency logistics.

6.1.3 *Case Study of China's Emergency Logistics: Wenchuan and Yushu Earthquakes*

On May 12, 2008, an 8.0 magnitude earthquake hit Wenchuan County, Sichuan Province, in Southwest China. Besides Sichuan, ten neighboring provinces such as Ganshu, Shaanxi and Chongqing also suffered damages of various degrees. The total area damaged by the earthquake was over 100,000 km^2; as many as 69,226 people were killed and 17,923 people were missing in this horrendous disaster.

On April 14, 2010, a 7.1 magnitude earthquake struck Yushu County of Yushu Tibetan Autonomous Prefecture, Qinghai Province; the earthquake's epicenter was located near the downtown of the county; as many as 2,698 people were killed and 270 people were missing in this incident.

Both earthquakes seriously damaged the infrastructures of traffic, water and power supply, and telecommunication in the disaster areas. The Wenchuan earthquake was the most severe earthquake since the founding of the PRC 60 years ago; it caused the most extensive damage and had the widest coverage, resulting in 845 billion RMB[4] of direct economic loss. Confronted with such a massive natural disaster, the Government adopted emergency measures, and emergency logistics played a very significant role in the quick response during this period of time. Table 6.1 provides a comparison of the two earthquakes.

Organizational assurance of emergency logistics

In both earthquakes, the principal participants in emergency logistics were multi-faceted, including chiefly government units, military forces and civil organizations. Following the earthquake, the State Council immediately designated the Commanding Office of Disaster Relief to lead, command and coordinate the emergency relief activities. The other departments of the Central Government and local

---

[4] "Special report on Wenchuan earthquake and disaster relief", Xinhua Net, September 11, 2008. http://news.xinhuanet.com/newscenter/2008-09/11/content_9923910.htm.

Table 6.1 Comparison of Earthquakes in Yushu and Wenchuan

	Yushu Earthquake	Wenchuan Earthquake
Time	07:49 a.m., April 14, 2010	02:28 p.m., May 12, 2008
Epicenter	Yushu County of Yushu Tibetan Autonomous Prefecture, Qinghai Province	Yingxiu Town, Wenchuan County, Sichuan Province
Intensity	About M7.1; about 30 km of fault zone	About M8.0; about 300 km of fault zone
Seismic region	Yushu County of Yushu Tibetan Autonomous Prefecture, Qinghai Province	Counties within 50 km of the epicenter and many large and medium-sized cities within 200 km of the epicenter
Areas affected	The earthquake affected some regions in Sichuan Province, especially Shiqiu County and Baiyu County	All regions in China except Heilongjiang, Jilin and Xinjiang experienced the shock; even Bangkok in Thailand, Hanoi in Vietnam, the Philippines and Japan also sensed the earthquake
Geography of seismic region	Yushu is a high-altitude region with high mountains; the average altitude is 4,493 m	Wenchuan is the world's largest geographical area with a typical topology of high mountains and deep gorges

(Continued)

Table 6.1   (*Continued*)

	Yushu Earthquake	Wenchuan Earthquake
Climate of seismic region	High temperature variability in seismic region; the severe snowstorm and strong winds in particular caused more difficulties for the disaster relief	The heavy rain and flood which occurred after the earthquake disrupted the disaster relief severely
Response level to the earthquake	Grade I (top grade, for most serious event)	Grade I (top grade, for most serious event)
Traffic of seismic region	800 km away from provincial capital, traffic was very inconvenient	Most of the roads were damaged in the earthquake; and due to the heavy rain afterwards, the risk of collapse covered the entire region
Telecom of seismic region	By 2:00 p.m., April 14, 2010, telecommunications for cabled phones and mobile phones to the seismic region were basically suspended	Both traffic and telecommunications to the seismic region were totally shut down; telecommunications in Chengdu city, the provincial capital, was basically suspended

Source: Compiled from the website of Global Times. http://www.huanqiu.com/zhuanti/china/qinghai7.1/.

governments such as the Civil Affairs, Finance, Commerce, Public Health, Transport, Civil Aviation, Public Security departments, and the military units, the All-China Red Cross Association and the China Charity Federation, actively participated in the relief activities, jointly contributing their efforts to the collection, delivery, receipt and release of emergency materials.

In addition, civil emergency logistics organizations played an important role in the relief effort; together with the Government these civil forces formed a new mode of participation. During the Wenchuan earthquake, the World Logistics Development and Promotion Organization and the China Charity Federation jointly established the Steering Group for China's Charity and Public Welfare Logistics on May 20, 2008, which consisted of two sub-sidiaries: China's Emergency Logistics Coordination Center and China's Emergency Rescue Center for Earthquake and Disaster Relief Logistics. Based on their previous experience in logistics organization, the Steering Group was responsible for the transmission, dispatch, delivery, management and other coordination of the disaster relief materials from charity and public welfare institutions. During the Yushu earthquake, Qinghai Logistics and Procurement Association fully contributed their organizational expertise, actively bearing the task of transporting and dispatching livelihood materials. For example, it safely and smoothly dispatched nearly 2,000 tons of livelihood materials to seismic regions within the first seven days to meet urgent needs and thereby offered great support to the people in distress.

Materials assurance of emergency logistics

After the two massive earthquakes, the Government immediately enacted its Grade I plan to cope with the disasters; meanwhile, all departments of the State Council, the General Staff Office of the People's Liberation Army, all provincial and municipal governments started their divisional, specific or regional plans. Governmental authorities and civil organizations cooperated to ensure the collection, dispatch, receipt and on-time distribution of disaster relief materials.

Furthermore, information about the disasters was released in time and publicly, affording active support to the social forces for gathering emergency materials, as well as guaranteeing their smooth delivery.

Garnering of emergency materials

Emergency materials for disaster relief were mainly for livelihood and medical treatment; the collection came from existing government disaster relief reserves, public donations and emergency procurement.

After the Yushu earthquake, China's National Development and Reform Commission immediately enacted the plan to allocate disaster relief grain reserves to the Yushu seismic region on April 16, 2010. It released 4,600 tons of grain reserves free-of-charge to the Yushu seismic region from the Central Reserve Warehouse, designating the Qinghai provincial government to organize the dispatch, processing and delivery of grain reserves, as well as distributing to the refugees freely. As a result, batches of emergency materials were delivered to the Yushu quake region within ten days, consisting of 57,000 tents, 117,000 coats, 207,000 quilts, 10,000 sets of ration food, 11,000 coal-heating furnaces, 20,000 folding beds, etc. After the Wenchuan earthquake, the Ministry of Commerce of the State Council effected the 24-hour emergency duty mechanism, keeping continual communication day and night with local commercial authorities in Shanghai, Tianjin, Henan, Hubei, Chongqing and other regions, thus ensuring the emergency dispatch and procurement of livelihood materials for the quake area. The Ministry of Civil Affairs received a total of 1.58 million tents, 4.86 million quilts, 14.10 million pieces of clothing, 3.77 million tons of fuel and 8.07 million tons of coal. Total public donations including sources from abroad to the quake region were valued at 59.38 billion RMB.[5]

---

[5] "Special report on anti-earthquake and disaster relief in Wenchuan earthquake", Xinhua Net, September 11, 2008. http://news.xinhuanet.com/newscenter/2008-09/11/content_9923910.htm.

Receipt and distribution of emergency materials

After the Wenchuan earthquake, in order to strengthen the management of disaster relief livelihood materials as well as to codify their allocation, distribution and use, the Ministry of Civil Affairs issued the *Measures for the Distribution of Disaster Relief Livelihood Materials in Wenchuan Earthquake* on June 1, 2008, stipulating specifically the principles, procedure and supervision for allocating, distributing and using the disaster relief livelihood materials for the Wenchuan earthquake.

Taking the Red Cross Society of China, Sichuan Branch, as an example, it received and distributed goods for the refugees' daily necessities, including mineral water, food, tents and quilts, as well as assisting apparatus or medicine for rescue actions. The workflow of material allocation is as shown in Figure 6.2. The disaster relief materials from all channels were transported to Chengdu by railway, highway, aviation, etc. These were registered by the reception group, stored and dispatched expediently under the command of the Materials Dispatching Center, then finally delivered to the quake region. The logistics information produced and required in all steps is monitored by the information center.

In view of the statistics on the delivered materials, most of the disaster relief materials received were dispatched to the quake region within a short time (as shown in Figure 6.3). This shows that the allocation mechanism for disaster relief materials is workable and that the distribution and use of materials can be monitored well under the system.

Analysis of the proportion of materials dispatched by regions shows that the Red Cross Society of China, Sichuan Branch, had basically distributed the disaster relief materials in proportion to the population size and the severity of disaster in the quake region (as shown in Figure 6.4). For example, according to the assessment of the quake regions, Qingchuan County, Guangyuan City, was rated as an extremely severe region, and other subordinate counties as very severe regions.[6] Consequently, the Red Cross Society of

---

[6] "About publishing the notice of evaluation to disaster scope in Wenchuan earthquake", website of the Ministry of Civil Affairs, China State Council. http://jzs.mca.gov.cn/article/zcwj/200808/20080800019056.shtml (original URL). http://wenku.baidu.com/view/3f90295f804d2b160b4ec0bc.html (working URL).

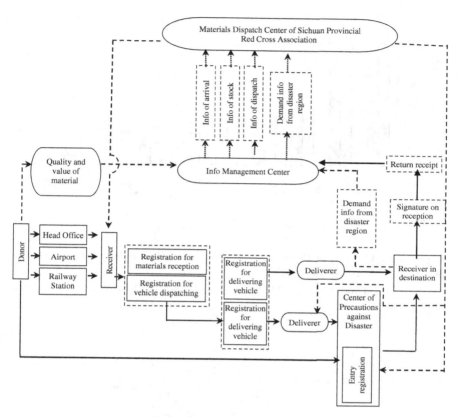

Figure 6.2 Dispatch Workflow of the Red Cross Society of China, Sichuan Branch, for Disaster Relief Materials

Source: Zhang Jin, "Analysis and thoughts on emergency logistics organization in Wenchuan earthquake", Emergency Logistics Summit Forum, China, August 2008.

China, Sichuan Branch, dispatched a high proportion of relief materials to these regions which had a large area and population. The distribution of disaster relief materials was in line with the principle of distributing the materials based on the acreage of the quake area, the severity of damage, the population density and the demand from refugees in the quake area, as stated in the *Measures for the Distribution of Disaster Relief Livelihood Materials in Wenchuan Earthquake*, issued by the Ministry of Civil Affairs of the State Council.

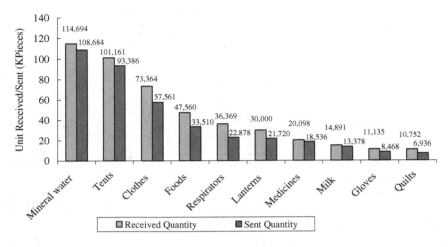

Figure 6.3 Quantity of Donated Materials Received/Dispatched by the Red Cross Society of China, Sichuan Branch

Source: Compiled from data released by the Red Cross Society of China, Sichuan Branch (as of July 14, 2008).

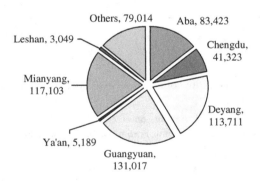

Figure 6.4 Units of Donated Materials Dispatched by the Red Cross Society of China, Sichuan Branch, by Regions

Source: Compiled from data released by the Red Cross Society of China, Sichuan Branch (as of July 14, 2008).

Transport assurance for emergency materials

After the disaster occurred, the rescue troops consisting of the PLA and policemen took quick action with the highest priority. The day after the Wenchuan earthquake, the PLA assigned 18 helicopters and 28 flights to airdrop 12.5 tons[7] of goods including food to the quake region. Ten minutes after the Yushu earthquake occurred, 850 PLA soldiers stationed in Yushu began rescue actions; in less than three hours, the first batch of rescue troops with 4,000 members set off to the quake region; within 11 hours, the state earthquake rescue troop with 110 members arrived at the seismic region; in 30 hours, the Central Government urgently dispatched 100,000 sets of field rations from stockpile warehouses to the seismic region.

Meanwhile, state transport management authorities, consisting mainly of the Ministry of Transport and the Ministry of Railways, started all emergency actions to ensure the safe and timely delivery of emergency materials to the quake region. After the Wenchuan earthquake, the Ministry of Railways announced that it was halting all other cargo to pre-empt the railroad resources, so as to make the best efforts to repair some parts of the main railway lines to Sichuan Province damaged in the earthquake, and to ensure the smooth delivery of disaster relief materials from the Materials Dispatch Center of the Red Cross Society of China, Sichuan Branch. Within 48 hours after the earthquake occurred, the Railway Department had dispatched 115 trains for 56,000 sets of tents and six trains for 283 lorries of oil to the quake region, as well as a huge amount of disaster relief food and medicines. The Ministry of Transport swiftly organized technical experts to arrive onsite the earthquake regions to guide and assist the restoration work; it also allocated a special fund to the local traffic and transport authority to support the repair of damaged highways and railways. After the Yushu earthquake, the Ministry of Railways immediately set up Dispatch and Command Rescue Stations, both in the Ministry of Railways and the Qinghai-Tibet Rail

---

[7] http://news.xinhuanet.com/newscenter/2008-05/13/content_8163460.htm, Xinhua Net.

Co., Ltd., which was responsible for round-the-clock actions of loading/unloading and delivery of relief materials, monitoring the information of materials delivery, guiding and supervising the local rail administrative bureaus in the entire process of speedy delivery of relief materials. Within 48 hours after the earthquake occurred, the Railway Department delivered a total of 18 trains of materials from Shenyang, Beijing, etc, to the quake region, including 750 tents, 50,000 overcoats and 37,000 quilts.

Furthermore, from the beginning of the rescue, air transport had played an important role in the delivery of emergency materials. For example, within five days after the Wenchuan earthquake, the General Staff Office of the PLA had drafted a total of 68 flights from Air China, China Eastern Airlines, China Southern Airlines, Hainan Airlines and China Western Airlines to deliver about 270 tons[8] of materials including medicines to the quake region within a short time.

Conclusions and notes

The Wenchuan and Yushu earthquakes represent unconventional and irregular events. After the occurrence of both earthquakes, the Chinese Government engaged the Grade I response, the top-class national response to public disaster, and adopted relevant emergency measures which were quite different from those for conventional and routine events. Rescue operations were commenced with active joint efforts between the Government and the people, saving people's lives and minimizing property loss as much as possible; meanwhile, the management of emergency logistics also contributed significantly.

In terms of organization and command, the Central Government responded quickly and established its leadership through its administrative power to pool the resources of all departments and channels. Local governments at all levels cooperated closely with the Central

---

[8] "Thoughts on calling plenty of civil aviation transport capabilities in Wenchuan earthquake", China Aviation Resources Net. http://news.carnoc.com/list/104/104781.html.

Government, coordinated all relevant departments and enterprises in carrying out the emergency logistics operations; the joint efforts led to the best synergistic benefits.

In view of channel capability, emergency materials and rescuers were transported to the quake region in a precise and timely manner within a very short period, thus improving the efficiency of emergency logistics and reducing the loss of lives and property to a minimum. For example, after the Wenchuan earthquake occurred, the geological condition became very precarious, e.g., landslides, damaged and blocked highways caused by mountains collapsing. The Chinese military forces adopted a combination of transport modes with airlifts as the most advanced and travel by foot as the most primitive to ensure uninterrupted emergency logistics.

But, generally speaking, some shortcomings still exist in China's emergency logistics.

First of all, the management system of emergency logistics still needs to be improved. Management of emergency logistics in China has been aimed at specific emergency events and only drafts people for specific emergency plans from different departments such as government agencies, military forces, civil affairs, public health, commerce, urban construction, traffic and transport. Thus shortcomings exist in many aspects — lack of a unified, highly effective and professional emergency dispatch mechanism, no good means of coordinating the logistics enterprises and the facility and distribution planning for emergency materials, no regular drills for organizing and commanding emergency logistics operations, etc.

Second, the infrastructure of emergency logistics needs to be improved. China has accelerated the construction of logistics parks, logistics centers and distribution centers, yet it lacks an overall consideration of the demand for emergency logistics or a comprehensive plan for the layout and functions of the nation's emergency reserve warehouse as well as the logistics centers and distribution centers. Hence, the emergency and regular logistics infrastructures are not formed into an organic unit. Moreover, the construction of regional integrated transport systems and channel systems lacks proper planning for the emergency logistics distribution channel. In some areas, the transport networks are few and scattered, and the reliability of local traffic and transport systems needs further improvement.

Third, the operating procedure for emergency logistics needs to be further optimized. Presently, in case of an emergency event, the logistics processes of packaging, storage, hauling, loading/unloading and transporting have not been scientifically programmed and designed in accordance with the purpose of emergency logistics. This results in many problems such as disparity between the label on the package and the information on the packing list, storage and stacking being inconvenient for mechanical operations, dispatching and scheduling of transport vehicles not meeting the requirements on speed, safety and economy.

Fourth, the level of informatization of emergency logistics is still low. The information management for emergency materials is impaired by shortcomings in many aspects: no standard classification for emergency materials, no unified and standard scheme to register, file and account for the information on the donation, receipt, distribution and use of emergency materials. These shortcomings tend to hinder the tasks of statistical compilation, inquiry, tracking, audit and supervision. Concerning the application of information technology in distribution, highly effective and modern technology for information collection and processing (e.g., RFID) still needs to be adopted.

Finally, the development and retention of emergency logistics talents needs further strengthening. Regarding professionals specializing in emergency logistics, the Government still needs to conduct more regular training for volunteers in professional knowledge and skills with regard to emergency rescue, while civil organizations should retain more professional talents to meet the need for emergency logistics when disasters occur.

6.2 Event Logistics: Beijing Olympic Games

Event logistics entails the flow of physical commodities caused by holding a large-scale activity, mainly including the distribution of consumption commodities, the transportation, storage and packaging of pre- and post-event related equipment and materials, information processing, as well as the disposal of waste generated from the activity.

Event logistics has particular features like complexity of demands, multiplicity of service objectives and staged timeframes. In 2008, the 29th Olympic Games was successfully held in Beijing. During this period, the Olympic Games logistics service played a very important role, offering fundamental support to the successful operation of the Beijing Olympic Games through its tight organization and management, scientific operation mode and robust security measures.

6.2.1 *Organization and Management of Beijing Olympic Games Logistics*

Macro organization and management

The logistics of the Beijing Olympic Games was based on a unique organization and management mode in which the Beijing Organizing Committee for the Olympic Games (hereinafter referred to as BOCOG) took the lead and all other departments cooperated and coordinated closely with it. Under this mode, BOCOG was the direct leader in the entire Olympic Games logistics operations, conducting integrated and unified allocation of labor, funds and property. The logistics department under BOCOG was chiefly responsible for the planning, management and procurement of Olympic Games materials, as well as offering logistics services. Governmental authorities such as the General Administration of Sports, the Ministry of Commerce, the General Administration of Customs and the Ministry of Transport were responsible for setting the relevant policies and regulations regarding the Olympic Games sporting activities; and drafting laws and regulations on domestic trading and investment by foreign enterprises, bidding quotas for import and export commodities, and guidelines on logistics for Olympic Games materials handled by highway, waterway or other transportation industries. They were also responsible for the entry and exit of Olympic Games materials, such as customs supervision, customs declaration and duty exemption, statistics, inspection for smuggling and management of ports. Figure 6.5 depicts the organizational structure and the main responsibilities of the government authorities for BOCOG.

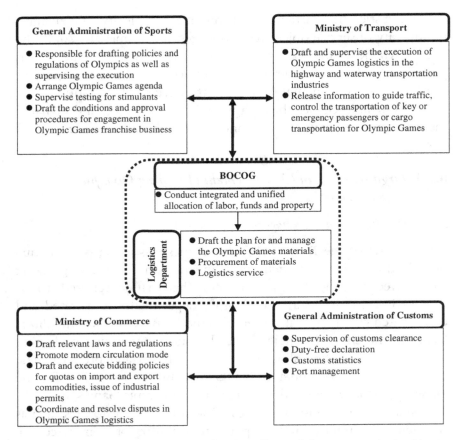

Figure 6.5   Management and Coordination Chart of Government Authorities in Beijing Olympic Games Logistics

Source: Luo Wei, Liu Zhixue, Sun Yongli, "Realization of coordinated logistics in Beijing Olympic Games", *China Logistics and Procurement*, 2007(11).

Micro execution and management

In terms of micro execution and management, the BOCOG Logistics Department was responsible for drafting the general plan for the Olympic Games materials and the specific plan for materials required by the stadiums, organizing the logistics team to serve the stadiums, procuring, storing and distributing materials for the Olympic Games and Paralympic Games, as well as offering other logistics services to the stadiums.

The BOCOG Logistics Department consisted of one general affairs office and three business offices, namely the General Office, Procurement Office, Logistics Office and Property Management Office, with their chief duties as shown in Figure 6.6.

Pursuant to BOCOG's unified arrangement and different tasks in various phases of materials assurance, the function and organization structure of the BOCOG Logistics Department also changed accordingly. While the focus of tasks gradually moved towards the stadium, the organization structure of each phase is as follows.

Planning phase (end of 2006 to March 2007)

In the planning phase, the organization structure mainly consisted of the four BOCOG functional departments and two cross-divisional teams for the stadium logistics project, which were responsible for drafting the policies, rules and standards as well as following the list of tasks and schedule to finish the preparation of stadium logistics.

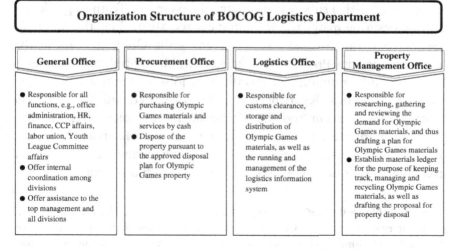

Figure 6.6 Organization Structure of BOCOG Logistics Department

Source: Compiled from the *Manual for Probationer in Olympic Games Logistics*.

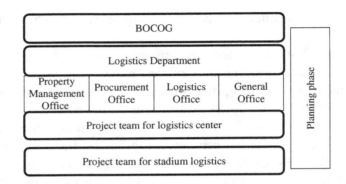

Figure 6.7   Model of Logistics Organization and Management for the Planning Phase

Source: Compiled from the *Manual for Probationer in Olympic Games Logistics.*

The organization structure of four offices plus two project teams and the detailed model of logistics organization and management in this phase are as shown in Figure 6.7.

Testing and adjustment phase (April 2007 to May 2008)

A separate committee was established for the "Good Luck Beijing" test events,[9] with a subordinate Materials Assurance Team to guide the tasks of ensuring materials for the test events. Meanwhile, the Materials Assurance Team also had a subordinate — the Guiding Team of the Stadium Logistics Project — to be responsible for training the testers by batch, and arranging and coordinating jobs for the test events. The BOCOG Logistics Department actively cooperated with the BOCOG Financial Department and the Marketing Development Department, and communicated and coordinated with the Materials Assurance Team to draft relevant policies on materials assurance for the test events, to guide and coordinate with the stadiums; but it did not

---

[9] The "Good Luck Beijing" test events were held by BOCOG under the requirement of the International Olympic Committee and its commitment in its application. From August 2006 to June 2008, a series of sports matches were held in all Olympic Games stadiums, in order to test and inspect the stadiums for their infrastructure, technical system, scheme and plan, operational guidelines and security capability.

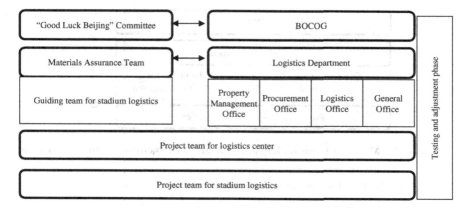

Figure 6.8 Model of Logistics Organization and Management for the Testing and Adjustment Phase

Source: Compiled from the *Manual for Probationer in Olympic Games Logistics.*

conduct any specific logistics management operations. The detailed model of logistics organization and management in this phase is as shown in Figure 6.8.

Operational phase (June 2008 to September 2008)

The Head of the BOCOG Logistics Department, acting as Director of the Logistics Center, was responsible for commanding key logistics operations; the Deputy Head, acting as Vice Director of the Logistics Center, was mainly in charge of the daily duties of the Logistics Office, and was responsible for the management of specific operations such as storage and distribution. Guiding teams for stadium logistics and non-competition stadiums were established to instruct and manage the logistics of competition and non-competition stadiums. A detailed model of logistics organization and management in this phase is as shown in Figure 6.9.

6.2.2 *Operating Model of Beijing Olympic Games Logistics*

In order to minimize the burdens of disposal and relocation after the Beijing Olympic Games, as well as to fully utilize the existing resources,

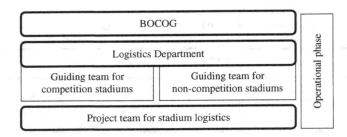

Figure 6.9   Model of Logistics Organization and Management for the Operational Phase

Source: Compiled from the *Manual for Probationer in Olympic Games Logistics.*

the logistics of the Beijing Olympic Games mirrored the successful operating model of logistics for the previous Olympic Games, relying on the Olympic Games Logistics Center to construct a highly effective operating system; while outsourcing detailed logistics operations to the sponsors and service suppliers.

Olympic Games logistics center

The Olympic Games Logistics Center, as the operations hub for Beijing Olympic Games logistics, was responsible for offering logistics services to competition, non-competition and training stadiums. The Center adopted an operating model with the following: site selection by the Government, base acquisition through bidding, investment by enterprises and leasing by the BOCOG Logistics Department. The organization structure of the Center conformed to the unified requirements by BOCOG for non-competition stadiums and accorded with the actual conditions for logistics operations. During the initial preparation stage, the Center used the model of combining the Preparation Team and the Ambient Assurance Team to carry out its work. After the Center commenced operations, it worked with the Stadium Running Team and the Ambient Assurance Team.

The operations system of Beijing Olympic Games logistics mainly included three procedures: customs clearance, distribution and recycling of the Olympic Games materials. The detailed operations workflow is shown in Figure 6.10.

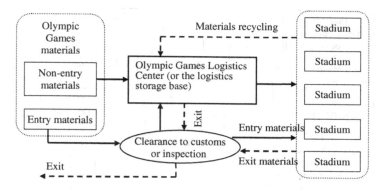

Figure 6.10   Operations Workflow of Beijing Olympic Games Logistics

Entry of Olympic Games materials

Customs clearance of Olympic Games materials included the document type and the non-document type. Non-document type clearance included clearance at seaports and airports, so clearance workflows for different materials would exhibit certain differences. For entry through seaports, the relevant Olympic Games materials would be delivered to the seaport by international vessels, and then Schenker China Ltd., the sole international freight and customs clearance agent for BOCOG, would be responsible for customs clearance. Schenker China Ltd. adopted a cross-customs model to deliver the materials directly to Beijing. After passing customs clearance and procedures for inspection and quarantine in the Beijing Olympic Games Logistics Center, the materials would be stored in the Center or transferred to the relevant stadiums on demand.

For entry through airports, the Grade I ground agent, such as an aviation ground services company, would first check the airway bills against the cargo; then transfer the airway bills to the customs clearance agent to clear the Olympic Games materials. Then the customs clearance agent would prepare the customs declaration form, invoice, packing list, certification issued by BOCOG and relevant documents for customs clearance. Upon completion of customs clearance and inspection and quarantine procedures, the Grade I ground agent would deliver the cargo to the Olympic Games Logistics Center. The

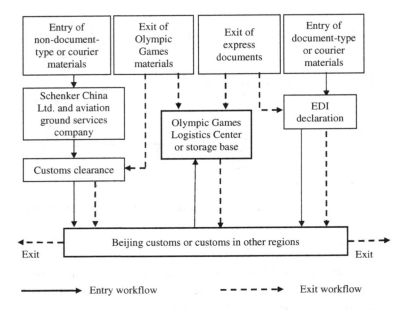

Figure 6.11   Workflows for Entry and Exit of Beijing Olympic Games Materials

detailed workflow for the entry and exit of Beijing Olympic Games materials is as shown in Figure 6.11.

All express documents or materials were cleared via EDI declaration in advance for speedy customs clearance, fast delivery and high efficiency. Normally, express documents would be cleared within 30 minutes; express cargo needed 40 minutes; while express items for exit needed 1.5 hours to clear customs.

Distribution of Olympic Games materials

The Olympic Games Logistics Center would distribute and recycle the materials to and from 31 competition stadiums and 15 non-competition stadiums in Beijing, including mainly competition apparatus, livelihood materials, Olympic Games mail, parcels and express items, newscast apparatus and waste.

Distribution management of Olympic Games materials consisted of three procedures, i.e., collection of users' requests, formulation of a general distribution plan and execution of distribution. First, the users with requests would log into the Transport Management System (TMS) module of the Olympic Games materials distribution system and submit their requests 48 hours in advance to the General Distribution Planning Team. Once the record entered the system, the system would automatically compile the requests into the general distribution plan. Upon approval and adjustment, the system would generate the data for entry, exit or exchange to every stadium. Finally, the system would carry out a precise calculation of the delivery times and routes of all vehicles upon referring to the traffic rules of the Olympic Games, then draft a timetable for distributing the Olympic Games materials. All drivers would follow the timetable to deliver the materials, pass through the security checks, as well as leave the stadium at the stated time, thus ensuring smooth circulation of materials among all stadiums.

In April 2008, BOCOG issued the *General Policy of Overall Distribution Plan,* stipulating that all distribution plans for competition or non-competition stadiums in Beijing would be scheduled and broadcasted only by the Olympic Games Logistics Center through the general distribution and planning system, rather than by the individual stadiums. For key sponsors or suppliers needing to distribute materials to multiple stadiums, they would communicate with the Center and submit, through a single designated contact person in charge of the general distribution plan, their general distribution requests to the Center; after receiving approval, they would not need to file requests through the stadiums.

Recycling of Olympic Games materials

During this phase, most of the recycled materials especially those for exiting, would first be stored in the key storage base or the Olympic Games Logistics Center, waiting for customs clearance and inspection and quarantine procedures. After going through customs clearance and inspection and quarantine procedures, they would be delivered to the designated port upon prior request, then shipped to the destination by sea or by air.

Information system for Olympic Games logistics

BOCOG adopted a supply chain model which designated one department to manage multiple functions in a unified way, covering procurement, logistics, property planning and management, and developed an Olympic Games logistics information system accordingly. The Olympic Games logistics information system consisted of four IT subsystems and one basic database: the Purchase Management System (PMS), the Warehouse Management System (WMS), the Assets Management System (AMS), the Distribution Management System (DMS) and the Logistics Basic Information Database. All the subsystems were interlinked to constitute an Olympic Games materials supply chain management system.

With any procurement by BOCOG, the materials must be entered into the PMS system for accounting; then the AMS system would take them into the property management section; after warehousing, the WMS system would manage the materials until they were handed out or distributed. At the last stage, the DMS system would be responsible for arranging the vehicles for transport. All vehicles entering the Olympic Games stadiums had to be registered in the system 48 hours in advance; afterwards, the DMS system, upon referring to the traffic rules during the time of the Olympic Games, would draft a timetable for logistics distribution for the vehicles.

Meanwhile, the information in the DMS would be synchronously transmitted to the relevant business nodes, thus to realize the optimized arrangement of the distribution plan and the most appropriate allocation of labor, equipment and resources.

In the Olympic Games logistics information system, UPS implemented the G-4 courier data collector (DIAD IV); after scanning a barcode, it could transmit the data immediately and then use the GPS technology to realize the integrated supply chain management of Olympic Games materials in procurement, storage and distribution.

Outsourcing of Olympic Games logistics

Beijing Olympic Games logistics employed the outsourcing model, entrusting the logistics business to UPS and Schenker China Ltd.

UPS was the sponsor of logistics and courier for the Beijing Olympic Games, specifically responsible for the duties of storing, allocating and distributing Olympic Games materials, and centrally managing the materials of the Center. It also carried out delivery and services for boat racing, canoeing and rowing competitions, and assisted BOCOG to draft and carry out the plan.

Schenker China Ltd. was responsible for offering international freight and customs clearance services to delegates from all countries, the International Olympic Committee (IOC), all international sports associations (federations), international broadcasting institutions, registered media, as well as the international freight service of sailboats. Beidun Co., Ltd. was the outsourced deliverer for transporting horses for the Olympic Games.

6.2.3 *Assurance Model of Beijing Olympic Games Logistics*

The highly effective operation of Beijing Olympic Games logistics should not only be attributed to the stringent organization and management and the scientific model for logistics operations. Other measures such as the efficient customs clearance model, traffic assurance model, food safety assurance model and property management model also afforded maximum assurance for the successful operation of Olympic Games logistics.

Customs clearance for Olympic Games materials

Concerning the customs clearance for Olympic Games materials, BOCOG and the General Administration of Customs jointly issued the *Customs Clearance Notice for Beijing Olympic Games Materials* and the *Measures by the General Administration of Customs to Support the Beijing Olympic Games* to stipulate policies for the entry and exit of all types of Olympic Games materials as well as a series of customs clearance policies.

Designated customs clearance ports and adjusted workflows

BOCOG designated Beijing Capital International Airport, Qingdao Liuting International Airport, Tianjin Binhai International Airport,

Shanghai Pudong International Airport, Shenyang Taoxian International Airport and Hong Kong International Airport to be its air freight ports; Qingdao, Tianjin, Qinhuangdao, Hong Kong and Shanghai to be the ocean freight ports. All Olympic Games materials entering via these ports would enjoy quick customs clearance. In addition, to speed up the customs clearance, other measures were taken, such as reforming the No. 3 aviation building of Beijing Capital International Airport and the east aviation building of Shanghai Pudong International Airport, adjusting the clearance workflow to "pre-classify, pre-declare, release first and collect tax afterwards", opening a special channel for customs declaration, and the 24-hour service.

Expansion of scope to use ATA Carnet

The ATA Carnet is an international customs clearance document used in many countries; it is also used in China as a temporary customs clearance procedure for the entry and exit of materials for exhibitions, fairs, conferences or similar activities. Accordingly, customers holding the ATA Carnet would enjoy the conveniences of being exempted from filling out the customs declaration form, paying the tariff and warranty deposit, applying for the permit for importing or exporting cargo, etc. For Olympic Games materials presented with the ATA Carnet, China's customs would offer a special entryway to the materials for bond and quick clearance. Otherwise, the applicant could apply for a Certificate of Entry for Olympic Games Materials in advance from the BOCOG Logistics Department, in which case customs would also accord the treatment per ATA Carnet standard.

Drafted series of customs clearance measures

In order to ensure the smooth and timely clearance of Olympic Games materials, China's local customs opened a "green entryway" for them, set up special-purpose windows and personnel, established a customs clearance ledger system for Olympic Games materials, offered service by appointment thereto, instituted a 24-hour emergency mechanism to deal with Olympic Games materials, conducted 24-hour customs clearance and offered 7-day, 24-hour services.

Strengthened customs supervision

BOCOG took the following measures related to customs supervision and safety of clearance:

First, it established the Security Examination Center for Olympic Games Materials; installed radioactivity detectors at frontier inspection stations of ports to prevent nuclear or radioactive materials from being imported or exported. Second, it made preparations for public emergencies and terrorism at the ports. Third, it strengthened the safety examination and approval procedures for importing food and health care products. Fourth, it strictly executed the quarantine and approval procedures for plant- and animal-related food, audited permits for transgenic food and audited licenses for health care products. Fifth, it strictly prohibited plant- and animal-related food imported from epidemic areas.

Food safety

Ensuring food safety during the Olympic Games was the most important determining factor in the success of the Beijing Olympic Games 2008. Since the Olympic Games was held during summer, the hottest season in the city, in order to ensure food safety, BOCOG adopted some stringent measures for Olympic Games food, for example, closed-loop supply chain management, end-to-end process tracking and a monitoring system, to ensure faultless food safety. Major security measures taken include the following.

Food tracking system

To establish a tracking system for Olympic Games food, BOCOG created a unified barcode system for all Olympic Games food, affixed electronic labels thereon, employed integrated technologies such as RFID, GPS, an automatic temperature and humidity recording and control system, and encrypted telecommunications. It also employed a unified barcode system for the delivery vehicles and the distribution operations. Meanwhile, it tracked and recorded the entire process for Olympic Games food from production to processing, transport and storage; set quality checkpoints at key nodes to conduct inspections and record the results; monitored the entire process from the origin of the food products to the processing enterprise, the logistics distribution center and the final consumption destination. All these helped to realize the traceability of Olympic Games food.

Cold chain logistics and information flow

GPS and automatic temperature recording equipment were used in the transport of Olympic Games food. Vegetables and meats needed were transported under refrigeration and the deliveries were made by following the specified routes strictly. While the food continually scattered and gathered when travelling from the suppliers to the end consumers, cold chain logistics and information flow was traced throughout the whole process at all times, thus ensuring the safe operation of the whole cold chain for Olympic Games food.

Multiple measures ensuring safe production and direct delivery

The production of Olympic Games food adopted the mode with specialized warehouses, production lines, labor, security protection and escorted vehicles to guarantee the safety of the food. For supply linkage, food processing enterprises distributed the food directly to the consumption locations, so as to reduce en route transshipping procedures and realize point-to-point delivery.

Traffic and transportation

Smooth traffic was another of the important factors to ensure the highly effective operation of Olympic Games logistics. It was also a great challenge to BOCOG, due to the overlapping of the irregular and complicated traffic of the Olympic Games and ordinary social traffic. Therefore, a combined model with both kinds of traffic was considered by BOCOG during the time of the Olympic Games, with the details as follows.

Improvement of traffic command system in Beijing

BOCOG improved the operations of the tri-level traffic command systems in the city center, district centers and centers for stadiums or key activity sites; improved the "122" emergency traffic call center; interlinked and interconnected three key computer networks for traffic command, CCTV surveillance, digital wireless cluster telecom and cabled telecom, thus enabling a high degree of integration of data, image and voice to offer a highly effective and unified traffic command service or escort service by police squad vehicles.

Proper allocation of transportation resources

BOCOG opened three 280 km designated Olympic Games lanes that helped to fulfill the commitment of a travel time of 30 minutes from residential locations to the stadiums; opened 34 Olympic Games city bus lines including ten express lines and 24 regular lines; added more bus lines at night to provide round-the-clock traffic smoothness; arranged more than 5,000 taxies to offer essential services to the areas neighboring the Athletes' Villages, the Media Village and the Olympic Games Park.[10]

Adoption of high-tech tools and intelligent system

Due to the huge coverage, diversity of clients' demands, large number and diverse origins of traffic service personnel, BOCOG established the command systems for large and small passenger vehicles, GPS

---

[10] Jia Shunping, "Some comments on Olympic and post-Olympic traffic — Record of the 4th China Traffic Top-Level Forum", *Journal of Transportation Systems Engineering and Information*, 2008.

surveillance system and telecom system. It adopted a wireless digital cluster system on a broad base, and reserved specific radio channels for communication with fleets. All these measures supported the highly efficient, smooth and flexible Olympic Games traffic operations.

Provision of comprehensive traffic information service

Owing to the event-related demand from Olympic competitions, measures for special traffic management had to be adopted. BOCOG had widely publicized these measures and offered a comprehensive inquiry service for Olympic Games traffic information through multiple media such as the Olympic Games website, outdoor information hall and LCD screens, electronic information terminals (TFT screens) at the public service hall of the traffic authorities, radio, television and newspapers.

Materials management

Beginning with procurement, the management of Olympic Games materials covered all the processes of warehousing and storage, serving the stadiums and delivery. All relevant information and lists produced from the logistics activities were entered into the Property Management System directly for property tracking management in all related steps, including delivery, arrival, pre-warehousing, storage, re-use, obsolescence and damage reporting.

The management model of Olympic Games materials adopted a tri-level responsibility system: the BOCOG Logistics Department was the leader and general controller; all responsible divisions coordinated specific management activities, and the users assumed the implementation obligations in practice. The materials management model adopted was partitioned by regions, objects and specialization, which resulted in a system of "unified management plus specific obligation". At the same time, according to the different categorization of Olympic Games materials, BOCOG adopted the "five unified principles", namely, unified planning, unified procurement, unified distribution, unified allocation and unified disposal, thus improving the efficiency and precision of property management.

6.3 China's International Trade Logistics

With the continuous development of global economic integration, China is increasingly becoming the world's most important manufacturing center and purchasing center. Along with the rapid growth, global trade logistics has become an important part of China's logistics market, and the international trade logistics service system is also being improved gradually.

6.3.1 *Major Types and Direction of International Trade in China*

With China's continual deepening integration into the global division of labor, the proportion of manufactured goods in China's export commodities has grown rapidly, while the proportion of primary products in China's import commodities continues to rise. So the direction of goods flow has also become increasingly complicated. The change in structure and direction of goods flow in China's international trade imposes higher requirements on the accuracy, timeliness, reliability and convenience of international trade logistics services.

Major types of goods

Before starting the reform and opening-up policies in the 1980s, China's international trade mainly focused on exporting raw materials, textile products and other primary products in the manner of general trade. Since the opening-up, with the rapid development of processing trade, the proportion of manufactured goods in China's export commodities has grown rapidly. By 2001, the figure had exceeded 90% and has continuously increased since then, while the proportion of manufactured goods in imported commodities dropped to under 70% in 2008.

Figures 6.12 and 6.13 show the main composition of China's export commodities and import commodities in 2008. It can be seen that mechanical equipment and light textile goods have become major parts of import and export commodities.

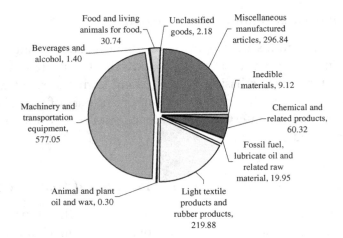

Figure 6.12   Main Composition of China's Export Commodities in 2008 (Unit: Billion USD)

Source: Compiled from the *China Statistical Yearbook* (2009), published by the National Bureau of Statistics of China, 2010.

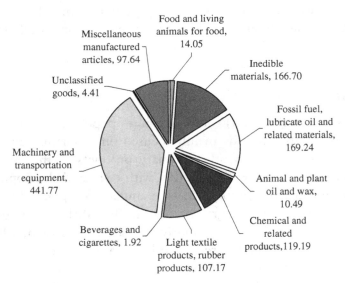

Figure 6.13   Main Composition of China's Import Commodities in 2008 (Unit: Billion USD)

Source: Compiled from the *China Statistical Yearbook* (2009), published by the National Bureau of Statistics of China, 2010.

Statistics for years 2000–2008 show that the value of China's primary products exported increased from 25.46 billion USD in 2000 to 77.96 billion USD in 2008, while the proportion decreased from 10.22% in 2000 to 5.45% in 2008. The value of industrial manufactured goods exported increased from 223.74 billion USD in 2000 to 1,352.74 billion USD in 2008; its proportion increased from 89.78% in 2000 to 94.55% in 2008, as shown in Figure 6.14.

Statistics for the same period also show that the value of primary products in imported goods increased from 46.74 billion USD in 2000 to 362.39 billion USD in 2008; while the proportion increased from 20.77% in 2000 to 32% in 2008. The value of industrial manufactured goods imported increased from 178.35 billion USD in 2000 to 770.17 billion USD in 2008; however, the proportion decreased from 79.23% to 68%, as shown in Figure 6.15.

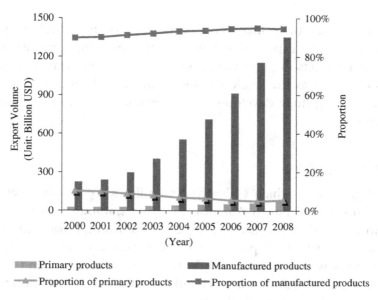

Figure 6.14 Change in Composition of China's Export Goods for 2000–2008

Source: Compiled from the *China Statistical Yearbook* (2009), published by the National Bureau of Statistics of China, 2010.

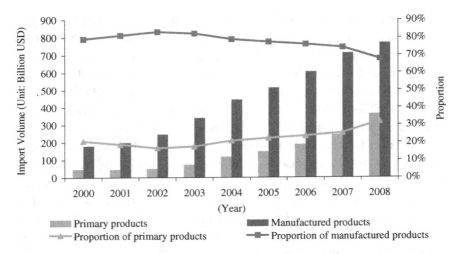

Figure 6.15   Change in Composition of China's Import Goods for 2000–2008

Source: Compiled from the *China Statistical Yearbook* (2009), published by the National Bureau of Statistics of China, 2010.

The substantially increasing proportion of industrial manufactured goods in export commodities and growing proportion of primary products in imported goods reflect the important characteristics of China as the world's manufacturing and processing center, and also bring huge development opportunities for China's international logistics.

Direction of goods flow

The regions with which China has trade flows are mainly located in Asia, Europe and North America; the main trading partners include countries and districts such as the US, Hong Kong, Japan, Korea and Taiwan. From China's perspective, the eastern coastal provinces are the regions with a relatively high proportion of import and export goods; the proportion of import and export goods in the central and western provinces is relatively low.

In 2008, the value of exports from China to Asia, Europe and North America was respectively 664.12 billion USD, 343.42 billion

USD and 274.27 billion USD, accounting for 46%, 24% and 19% of China's total exports. The total value of imports from the three regions to China was respectively 702.59 billion USD, 168.06 billion USD and 94.07 billion USD, accounting for 62%, 15% and 8% of China's total imports. Details are as shown in Figures 6.16 and 6.17.

Among China's major international trading partners, the countries or districts with a relatively high level of exports to China are the US, Hong Kong and Japan, those with a relatively high level of imports from China are Japan, Korea and Taiwan, as shown in Figures 6.18 and 6.19.

Among all provinces in China, those having a relatively high level of imports and exports are eastern coastal regions such as Guangdong, Shanghai and Jiangsu, as shown in Figure 6.20. The level of imports and exports for the Central and Western regions falls far behind; Tibet, Ningxia and Qinghai are among the provinces with the lowest import and export value, below the national average.

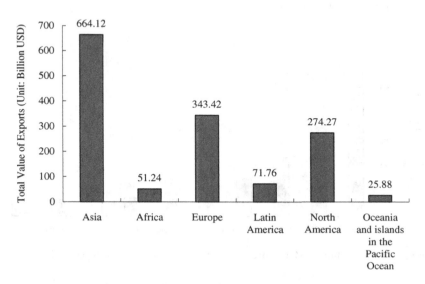

Figure 6.16　Regional Composition of China's Exports in 2008

Source: Compiled from the *China Statistical Yearbook* (2009), published by the National Bureau of Statistics of China, 2010.

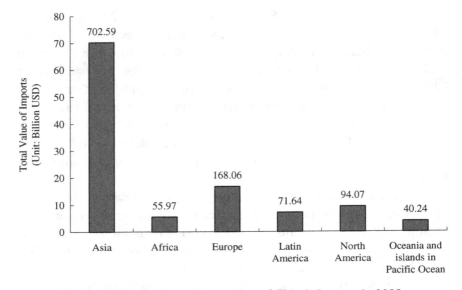

Figure 6.17   Regional Composition of China's Imports in 2008

Source: Compiled from the *China Statistical Yearbook* (2009), published by the National Bureau of Statistics of China, 2010.

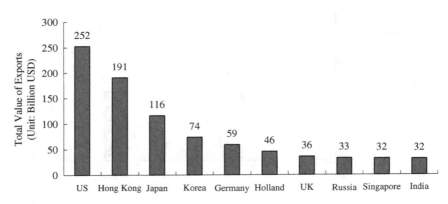

Figure 6.18   China's Main International Trade Export Countries and Values in 2008

Source: Compiled from the *China Statistical Yearbook* (2009), published by the National Bureau of Statistics of China, 2010.

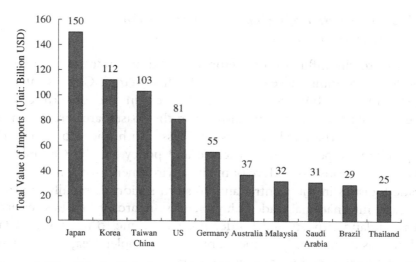

Figure 6.19 China's Main International Trade Import Countries and Values in 2008

Source: Compiled from the *China Statistical Yearbook* (2009), published by the National Bureau of Statistics of China, 2010.

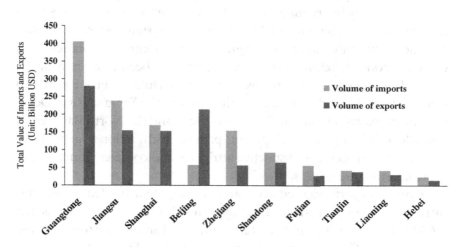

Figure 6.20 China's Top Ten Provinces in Terms of Import and Export Value in 2008

Source: Compiled from the *China Statistical Yearbook* (2009), published by the National Bureau of Statistics of China, 2010.

6.3.2 *Distribution of China's International Trade Logistics Business*

Subject to the influence of regional conditions, industrial structure, mode of economic development and other factors, China's international logistics business is mainly located in the eastern coastal regions; the major ports and airports in the coastal area are the main nodes of international logistics business. With the Government's expanding support in infrastructure and policy for the Central and Western regions, the development environment for international trade logistics in the Central and Western regions is rapidly improving, the international trade volume and standard of logistics services at the inland airports and border ports continue to improve. So far China has preliminarily formed a relatively complete sea, land and air international trade logistics service system.

Major ports

Statistics show that 90% of China's import and export volume are accounted for by international ocean transport, which plays an important role in China's international logistics service system. Most economic activities between China and foreign countries occur in the eastern and coastal regions, therefore ports in the regions have been extensively developed. These ports constitute five major port clusters. From north to south they are located in the Bohai Rim Region, the Yangtze River Delta, the Fujian coastal region, the Pearl River Delta and the North Bay region, basically exhibiting a development pattern with rational geographic placement, arrangement, distinctive attributes and complete functions, as depicted in Figure 6.21.

China's export-oriented economic development has led to the dramatic increase in port traffic. In 2009, China's total port traffic reached 7.66 billion tons, with eight coastal ports ranked among the top ten ports in the world. These ports are Shanghai, Ningbo, Tianjin, Guangzhou, Qingdao, Dalian, Qinhuangdao and Shenzhen, and the traffic of Shanghai Port continues to be ranked No. 1 in the world. By 2009, 20 out of 30 ports with a traffic of over 100 million tons were in China.

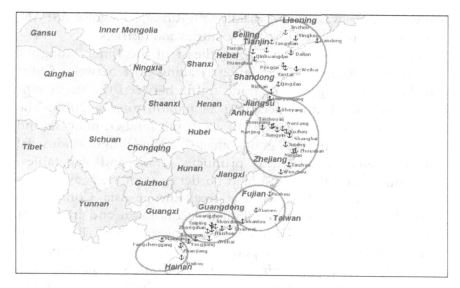

Figure 6.21   China's Five Major Port Clusters

With the increase of goods in foreign trade, container traffic at all of China's ports showed a stronger growth trend. In 2009, China's container goods traffic reached 122 million TEUs. Among the world's top 20 container ports in 2009, nine ports were in China, seven of which were in Mainland China. Five of China's ports — Shanghai, Shenzhen, Guangzhou, Ningbo and Qingdao — are among the world's top ten container ports.[11]

Major land border ports

China has a 22,800 km land border with 15 neighboring countries. So far there are 122 open land border ports, including Manzhouli, Erlianhaote, Alashankou, Huoerguosi and Pingxiang. International logistics services at China's land border ports are conducted through

----

[11] Ministry of Transport of China, *The Report on China's Shipping Development* (2009), China Communications Press, China, 2010.

highways and railways linking mainly with Russia, Mongolia, ASEAN, West Asia and other neighboring countries and districts.

Manzhouli, situated in the northeast of the Inner Mongolia Autonomous Region, is the largest trading port between China and Russia, bearing 60% of trade traffic between the two countries, with trade traffic exceeding 24 million tons in 2009. The imported goods mainly consist of crude oil, lumber, minerals and fertilizers; the exported goods mainly include light industrial products, electromechanical products, grain and vegetables. Manzhouli is also the largest land border port and railway port in China, and a vital hub for the first Europe-Asia Continental Bridge.[12] It is the most convenient, economical and important land and ocean international channel between China, Russia and Europe, with the traffic of goods topping other similar border ports in China. After opening its airport in 2005, Manzhouli has become an integrated international port with highway, railway and aviation capabilities.

Erlianhaote is the largest highway border port and the only railway border port between China and Mongolia; more than 70% of commodities imported from Mongolia enter China at Erlianhaote. In 2009, the traffic of goods through Erlianhaote Port reached 6 million tons; the main types of imported goods are coal, fuel, lumber and metallic ore. The main types of exported goods include steel, construction material, light industrial products, electromechanical products, grain and vegetables. Erlianhaote is the most expedient channel for China's railway to connect Europe and Asia; the railway between Beijing and Moscow by way of Erlianhaote is 1,140 km shorter than that through Manzhouli. Especially after

---

[12] Also called the Siberian Continental Bridge, it penetrates North Asia, from Khabarovsk and Vladivostok in east Russia, through the longest railway in the world — the Siberia Railway (Moscow to Vladivostok — to European countries, and finally to the Port of Rotterdam in the Netherlands. It spans 13,000 km, connecting the Pacific Ocean and the Atlantic Ocean, going through seven countries, including Russia, China, Kazakhstan, White Russia, Poland, Germany and the Netherlands.

Tianjin Port was connected to the railway network, it became an ideal channel for Japan, Southeast Asia and other neighboring countries to transship goods to Mongolia, Russia and East European countries; most importantly it is the sole channel for Mongolia to reach the ocean.

Alashankou and Huoerguosi are important border ports for China to open up to the Central Asian countries. Alashankou is the second largest land border port in China, as well as an important railway border port on the Second Europe-Asia Continental Bridge. In 2008, Alashankou Port realized 19 million tons of goods traffic. Imported goods through Alashankou mainly include metallic ore, steel (scrap steel), crude oil, chemical products, fertilizers; exported goods mainly consist of light industrial products, mineral construction material, industrial and engineering machinery and transit containers. Huoerguosi is the largest highway border port in Western China, and also one of the important border ports for China to trade with Central Asia and Europe. The major types of goods that go through Huoerguosi Port include cow and sheep skin, carpets, crude oil products, apparel, construction material, food, home appliances as well as furniture, automobiles and machinery.

Pingxiang Port is the only border railway port in Guangxi Province, the most convenient railway channel for China to connect with ASEAN, and an important window for the China-ASEAN free trade zone. The major types of goods that go through Pingxiang Port include fruits and vegetables, grain, light industrial products and electromechanical products.

Major airports

In recent years, China has experienced relatively extensive growth in airborne logistics business, with international airborne business also on the rise. By 2009, China had 166 (approved) civil airports (not including Hong Kong, Macao and Taiwan, the same hereinafter), 165 of which are aerial liner airports connecting 163 cities. In 2009, China's international airline saw 3.2 million tons of goods traffic, and

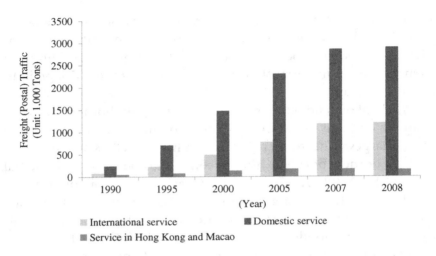

Figure 6.22   China's Air Freight (Postal) Traffic in Recent Years

Source: Compiled from the *China Statistical Yearbook* (2009), published by the National Bureau of Statistics of China, 2010.

the take-offs and landings of international flights reached 367,000.[13] Recently, China's airborne logistics business has been increasing by the year, and international airborne business is also up. Changes in China's air freight (postal) traffic are shown in Figure 6.22.

So far, the top ten airports in Mainland China in terms of air freight traffic are Shanghai Pudong, Beijing Capital, Guangzhou Baiyun, Shenzhen Bao'an, Shanghai Hongqiao, Chengdu Shuangliu, Kunming Wujiaba, Hangzhou Xiaoshan, Nanjing Lukou and Xiamen Gaoqi, among which Shanghai Pudong ranks No. 6 in the world. Of all the airports, 44 airports have an annual freight and postal traffic of over 10,000 tons, with their total freight and postal traffic accounting for 98.83% of all the airport traffic. The nation's freight and postal traffic is mainly distributed in the eastern and coastal regions; the volume of traffic for Beijing, Shanghai and Guangzhou account for 57.42% of the total.

---

[13] *2009 National Airport Production Statistics Report*, Civil Aviation Administration of China, 2010.

6.3.3 *International Trade Logistics Service Provider*

Ocean transport as the major means of international goods transport dictates that shipping companies are the chief providers of China's international trade logistics services. The ocean transport industry is also one of the markets with the highest degree of openness in China; multinational logistics enterprises backed by internationally known shipping companies have become a major part of China's international ocean transport logistics market. After China joined the WTO in 2001, the international air transport logistics market was further opened, and large international express delivery enterprises have been accelerating their entry into China's market.

Major international ocean transport logistics enterprises

China adopts a completely open policy towards the business practice of foreign ocean transport companies at all its open ports. By the end of 2009, there were about 140 international liner and transport enterprises in China and 3,507 non-vessel operating carriers; foreign companies established 40 solely owned shipping companies and 186 subsidiary companies in China; foreign companies established seven solely owned container transport service companies and 73 subsidiary companies.

The rapid growth of international logistics business has created excellent conditions for the development and strengthening of the ocean transport industry in China. By the end of 2009, China had an ocean transport fleet of 102 million deadweight tons, accounting for 8.3% of the transport fleet in the world, ranking fourth behind Greece, Japan and Germany. Major Chinese shipping companies engaged in international ocean transport business include COSCO, CSCL and SINOTRANS. Among them COSCO has a total shipping capacity of 770 ships and 53.07 million deadweight tons, and ranks first in terms of total scale; SINOTRANS and CSCL have fleets of 20.18 million deadweight tons and 11.27 million deadweight tons respectively, ranking second and third.

Major international air transport logistics enterprises

Since the mid-1990s, air freight has been rapidly developing globally. The annual average growth rate of China's air freight even reached 10%, which is far higher than the world's air freight growth rate of 6%; the growth in international freight traffic volume is especially fast. But since China's commercial air transport business started late, airline companies generally paid little attention to the freight business; the proportion of international air freight traffic for Mainland Chinese airline companies continues to decline. Although China has become the second-largest air transport country in the world, there is still no Mainland Chinese airline company among the top ten global airline companies in terms of international freight traffic. According to statistics published by the International Air Transport Association, the proportion of Chinese airline companies in the international air freight market has declined from 65.6% in 1995 to less than 30% in 2009; the volume of China's international air freight carried by foreign airline companies has been rising continually.

At Shanghai Pudong International Airport, the golden market for China's international air freight, the volume handled by foreign carriers accounted for 87% of the total air freight traffic in 2008. Meanwhile, international air express delivery giants and air freight companies are still accelerating their expansion into China's international air freight market. For example, UPS established an express operation center at Shanghai Pudong International Airport, and signed an agreement in 2008 with Shenzhen Airport to move its Asia-Pacific operation center from Clark Airport in the Philippines to Shenzhen Airport. FedEx established its transshipment center in China at Hangzhou Xiaoshan Airport in 2007; it also finished the construction of the Guangzhou Baiyun Airport Asia-Pacific Transshipment Center which officially began operations in 2009.

Integration trend of international trade logistics services

In traditional international logistics operations, the goods owner often outsources the transport, reservation, distribution placement and customs declaration to international forwarding companies, unloading companies, transport brokers and other agents. International logistics operations require many specific institutions to work as agents for the owner enterprise in carrying out each part of the international trade logistics service. Therefore international trade logistics service providers include many traditional industries such as shipping companies, airline companies, warehousing enterprises, yard companies, international forwarding enterprises, customs brokers and comprehensive logistics service enterprises. The increasing internationalization of production and enterprise supply chain management places even higher requirements on international trade logistics services. Since goods owners hope to outsource all the business to one company, third-party international logistics companies providing integrated services continue to appear in China's international logistics market and many large traditional shipping enterprises are also transforming into integrated logistics service suppliers.

Maersk Logistics Company, established in 2000, is a supply chain company belonging to the AP Moller Group. It provides customers with customized logistics solutions, including integrated supply chain management, storage and distribution, ocean transport and air transport services. Oriental Overseas Container Line (OOCL) has already announced its intention to be the most outstanding and most creative container transport and logistics service provider. American Presidents Lines (APL) has established Jimei Logistics Company to provide full-scale supply chain logistics services; COSCO and CSCL have also established their own logistics companies to provide goods owners with integrated logistics services.

6.3.4 *Facilitation of China's International Trade Logistics*

In 2009, China's imports and exports totaled 2.2 trillion USD, including 1.2 trillion USD of exports and 1.0 trillion USD of imports; its value of exports ranked first in the world. The rapid growth of international trade places higher requirements on the standard of international trade logistics services. In this regard, each level of government in China has issued a series of policies and plans to promote and develop international logistics services, resulting in a notable improvement of the policy environment and infrastructure for the development of international logistics.

Free trade agreement

With the trend of economic globalization, regional free trade zones play an important role and have become important means for all countries to expand foreign economic cooperation and promote economic development. With the increasingly closer trade relationship China has with the world, the regional free trade agreements between China and other regions in the world are also increasing. In recent years, the Chinese Government signed the agreement for joining the WTO (2001). China as an entity signed the *Mainland/Hong Kong (Macao) Closer Economic Partnership Arrangement* in 2003, the *China-ASEAN Free Trade Agreement* in 2002, the *China-Chile Free Trade Zone Agreement* in 2005 and the *Economic Cooperation Framework Agreement* with Taiwan in 2010.

The multilateral agreements under the WTO framework and regional integration bilateral free trade zone agreements will have a dual impact on China's international trade logistics. On the one hand, they will afford China a closer economic relationship with the world, and create for China and other countries, especially those free trade agreement partners, a large demand for commodity logistics. On the other hand, foreign enterprises will take the opportunity to enter China's market and engage in international trade logistics operations as well, further accelerating the competition in China's international logistics market.

Border port environment

Grand customs clearance

In 2002, the Chinese Government began the full promotion of the grand customs clearance system in border port logistics; various levels of customs and border port administration departments, based on their actual conditions, put forth detailed measures for the grand clearance tasks. Step by step they promoted the implementation of the grand clearance system, and achieved marked progress in enhancing border port customs efficiency, optimizing the border port logistics procedures, and the construction of electronic border ports, etc.

In implementing the grand clearance system, China's customs issued four kinds of new customs models: the convenient clearance model, the fast clearance model, the computer network monitored clearance model and the paperless clearance model. During the entire process from the customs clearance service by the import or export owner, to collecting imported goods or shipping the export goods to the custodial area, the border port administration department uses information technology and high-tech means to integrate the document flow, commodity flow, fund flow and information flow required in customs, so as to realize the administration department's objectives in effective monitoring and providing highly efficient services.

Inspection and quarantine department

In the implementation of the grand clearance system, the inspection and quarantine department and customs actively coordinated with each other to further improve the customs system and reform the epidemic inspection and monitoring model, and attained good progress in process acceleration, burden relief, efficiency enhancement and monitoring enforcement. In order to meet the requirements of the grand clearance system, the epidemic inspection department changed its traditional post-inspection/declaration model to a model with advanced declaration, advanced approval of import document and attachments, and advanced analysis of diseases or epidemics abroad.

Electronic border port

Starting from 2000, the Chinese Government began to construct an electronic law enforcement system for border ports, the China Electronic Border Port, for the purpose of employing modern information technology and using state telecommunication public network resources to integrate the information flow, fund flow, goods flow and the electronic accounting data involved in border port administration and law enforcement. The system encompasses foreign trade, customs, industry and commerce, taxation, foreign exchange and transport in one public data center. As data sharing and exchange are realized in a unified, complete and highly efficient computer network, border port administration and law enforcement departments are able to make cross-department and cross-industry data exchanges and network data inspections. It will also permit enterprises to execute customs clearance, declarations, settlements, export tax rebates and various other import and export operations on the network. So far, China's electronic border port system is being tested at the border ports in Beijing, Tianjin, Shanghai and Guangzhou.

Continuous improvement of bonded logistics system

For a long time, China's foreign exports were of a general trading type, but in recent years processing trade has emerged. As shown by statistics published by China's Customs Administration, processing trade accounted for 49% of total export value and 32% of total import value in 2009; processing trade is gaining significance in China's foreign trade sector. Bonded logistics, as a vital supporting platform for China to engage in the international division of industries, is the necessary link in completing the import/export step of the processing trade. The development of bonded logistics is indispensable to the expansion of the trade zone and the industrial scale of processing trade.

Bonded logistics refers to a kind of logistics required inside the custodial special zone and between different zones, involving warehousing, distribution, transport, circulation and processing, loading and shipping, logistics information and other functions. Through bonded logistics operations, enterprises can enjoy the "within border, outside customs" system and other special policies in taxation, foreign exchange and customs clearance.

So far, China has established a bonded logistics customs system with the bonded port area and comprehensive bonded area as the core, bonded logistics zone and bonded logistics center as the hub, and the widespread export custodian warehouses and bonded warehouses as the network nodes. Each type of bonded logistics custodial zone has different functions and policies, as shown in Table 6.2.

Table 6.2 Comparison of Different Types of Bonded Logistics Custodial Zones

Model	Location	Function	Logistics Management Model and Operation Entity	Tax Rebate Policy	Approval Authority
Bonded warehouse	Not limited	Handles bonded goods specifically for import or export and other goods without customs procedures	Operated by multiple enterprises	None	Directly governed by customs
Export custodial warehouse	Not limited	Undertakes functions in warehousing, bonded logistics distribution, provides value-added services via circulation	Operated by multiple enterprises	Part of the warehouse enjoys the immediate tax rebate after entering the warehouse	Directly governed by customs
Bonded logistics center (A)	Set in seaports, airports, land communication hubs and inland places with large demand for international logistics, a customs institution and convenient for centralized customs monitoring	Integration, optimization and enhancement of bonded warehouse and export monitoring warehouse. It provides circulation processing value-added and services, global purchasing and international bulk-breaking distribution service, export trade and	Constructed and operated by the same enterprise	Tax rebate made after entering the centre	General customs administration

(*Continued*)

Table 6.2   (*Continued*)

Model	Location	Function	Logistics Management Model and Operation Entity	Tax Rebate Policy	Approval Authority
		international transfer business and other international logistics business functions approved by customs, where the bonded warehousing period for goods in the logistics center is two years			
Bonded logistics center (B)	Same as bonded logistics center (A)	Same as bonded logistics center (A)	Operated by one enterprise, multiple enterprises enter and engage in bonded logistics business	Tax rebate made after entering the centre	General customs administration
Bonded logistics park	Established in the planned bonded area or the special port zone neighboring the bonded area	Relies on the bonded area and port, using the functional advantage of the bonded area and port, to develop a direct clearance channel between the park and the port area, implement a fast exit clearance procedure for	The administration entity is the administrative committee of the bonded area; the actual operation is carried out by the commodity owner and the third-party logistics company	Tax rebate after entering the zone	The State Council

(*Continued*)

Table 6.2 (*Continued*)

Model	Location	Function	Logistics Management Model and Operation Entity	Tax Rebate Policy	Approval Authority
		batches and centralized declaration. The zone focuses on logistics functions; it has no processing or manufacturing function; no warehousing term is made for goods in the park			
Bonded area	Around seaports	Import and export processing, international trade, bonded warehousing, commodities exhibition and others	Same as for bonded logistics park	Tax rebate made after crossing the border	The State Council
Export processing area	Not limited	Usually only has the functions of processing, manufacturing, assembly, warehousing; the expanded export processing area also has the functions of bonded goods flow, R&D, testing, maintenance business	Operated by multiple enterprises	Tax rebate made after entering the zone	The State Council

(*Continued*)

Table 6.2   (*Continued*)

Model	Location	Function	Logistics Management Model and Operation Entity	Tax Rebate Policy	Approval Authority
Bonded port area	Around seaports	Border port operation, international transfer, international distribution, international purchasing, export trade, bonded processing, import and export commodities exhibition, commodities service transaction, investment and financing insurance	Managed by the administrative committee of the port area, actually operated by the commodity owner and the third-party logistics company	Tax rebate made after entering the zone	The State Council
Comprehensive bonded area	Inland area	Same as bonded port area	Same as bonded port area	Same as bonded port area	The State Council

Development Prospects of the Logistics Industry in China

With the continual spread of the global financial crisis in 2009, China's economy was affected severely. The Chinese Government instituted aggressive financial policies and moderately relaxed monetary policies, implemented and improvised a package of plans to counter the financial crisis, and thus realized an economic recovery ahead of the rest of the world. Meanwhile, the issuance of the *Logistics Industry Adjustment and Revitalization Plan* boosted the confidence of the logistics industry, resulting in a positive outlook for the development of the logistics industry.

On the market demand side, the demand for international logistics sank, but the domestic demand for logistics maintained a steady growth. In particular, the market demand of the automobile and home appliance industries experienced a huge growth. On the supply side, owing to the sluggish demand and rising operating costs, many logistics firms had lackluster performance; many local firms began engaging in market consolidations, and some foreign-funded businesses moved aggressively into the emerging market segments. For infrastructure, the Government greatly expanded the scope of construction, injecting record-high investments in many areas, leading to a sizable expansion of the overall logistics infrastructure.

Akin to the economic development, the logistics development in China has exhibited typical regional disparities. The Eastern region has a massive logistics demand, especially for international logistics, is well-endowed with transportation infrastructure and more advanced logistics enterprises, and has a better customs custodial system and rapidly developing port logistics. The logistics development of the Western region is lagging behind that of the Eastern region. Nevertheless, the construction of transportation infrastructure has been noticeably accelerated, its inland waterway logistics has made significant contribution, and many logistics enterprises have made their move westward.

Specialized logistics enterprises in industries such as chain retail, automobiles, petroleum and electronic products are developing rapidly. The scale of chain retail logistics has grown swiftly, with a higher proportion of consolidated delivery. Privately operated distribution centers of enterprises still make up the majority, yet supplier-managed logistics and third-party logistics are gaining ground. The chain retail industry is facing a more advantageous policy environment. The demand for automobile logistics has grown, and the construction of infrastructure for automobile logistics has accelerated, leading to fast development of the logistics industry. Petroleum logistics has evolved so that state-owned, private- and foreign-invested modes of business co-exist, along with self-operating and third-party modes of business. The logistics demand of electronic and information products keeps growing, and the need for return logistics is also rising. Regional logistics centers are beginning to appear; the network of third-party logistics is maturing; and the Internet direct-sale model has simplified the path of logistics.

In recent years, several hot logistics issues in China have attracted global attention. China has attained greater achievement in emergency logistics, event logistics and international trade logistics. Following the Wenchuan and Yushu earthquakes, China established its emergency logistics management system. During these disaster events, the organizational command responded swiftly to the emergency, the Government coordinated the emergency logistics operations of various departments and relevant enterprises in a timely fashion, and effected the cooperative efforts. Better channel capability allowed timely and accurate transport of emergency materials and rescue personnel, raising the efficiency of emergency logistics and minimizing the loss of lives and property. The Beijing Olympics was held with great success. The tight organization, the scientific operational mode and fortified security measures of the Olympics logistics provided a solid foundation for the successful performance. And with the rapid expansion of international trade, international trade logistics has become a significant component of China's logistics market. The international trade logistics service system has also become more advanced.

2010 was a pivotal year as China continued to deal with the international financial crisis, maintain stable and rapid development of the economy and speed up the transitional economic development. It was also important since the *Logistics Industry Adjustment and Revitalization Plan* was implemented. With the global economy gradually stepping out of the financial crisis in 2011, development of logistics in China will face a bright future along with the slow recovery of the global economy and the rapid development of China's economy. Aspects germane to this perspective are summarized in the following paragraphs.

7.1 Continual Recovery of Total Logistics Value

In 2010, China continued to actively implement its financial policy and flexible monetary policy, carry out structural tax-cutting policies, increase domestic demand, promote the adjustment of the economic structure, as well as maintain the continuity and stability of ongoing policies. China's GDP increased by 10.3% in 2010. Against this macroeconomic background, the total value of social logistics in 2010 increased by 15%, the added value of the logistics industry reached more than 13.1%, while the proportion of the total expenses of social logistics in GDP continued to decrease.[1]

---

[1] National Logistics Information Network. http://dx88.56888.net/news/2010129/486025261.html.

7.2 Further Adjustment of the Structure of the Logistics Market

In 2010, while China maintained stable and rapid growth of the national economy, accelerating the transition of economic growth and adjustment of the economic structure has become the theme of economic development in China. The consumption, industrial, regional, urban and rural structures are changing noticeably; the demand structure, regional structure and industrial structure of the logistics market will be greatly affected, and the demand for logistics service quality will be further raised.

7.3 Condition of International Logistics Market Remains Severe

In 2010, the pace of global economic growth remained slow, the recovery unbalanced, and the conditions for continuing growth fragile. While recovery in the majority of advanced economies continued to be sluggish, most new emerging economies and developing economies have shown signs of greater growth driven by strong domestic demand.[2] As such, the major advanced economies are still unable to afford strong support for global economic growth in the upcoming period, the risk in the financial arena has not been thoroughly eliminated and protectionism in global trade has been fortified.

The global economic recovery, albeit weak, has to some extent improved the external environment for economic growth and promoted the recovery of China's foreign trade. However the demand in the international market remains soft and the situation facing China's international logistics market is still severe.

7.4 Continual Growth in the Demand for Domestic Logistics

In 2010, the home appliance and automobile industries received active policy support; the steel, cement and real estate sectors

---

[2] "Global economic prospects", International Monetary Fund, 2010. http://www.imf.org/external/chinese/pubs/ft/weo/2010/update/01/pdf/0110c.pdf.

remained hot spots in the economy; and strategic high-tech industries, including new energy, new material, energy-saving and
environment-protecting, biomedicine, information network and
high-end manufacturing, were also developed. As a supporting service industry for the home appliance, automobile, steel, cement and
other industries, the logistics industry has gained more business due
to the expanded market.

The development of China's rural logistics market deserves
attention. In 2010, besides continually implementing and improving the subsidy policy for automobiles and domestic appliances in
rural areas, China further adopted various farmer-benefiting measures to boost farmers' incomes and propel the construction of the
rural logistics system. The demand in the rural logistics market is
expected to increase and the overall scale is expected to grow further beyond 2010.

7.5 Enlarging Sphere of Cross-Strait Logistics Cooperation

The *Economic Cooperation Framework Agreement* (ECFA) signed in
2010 was an external trade agreement of the broadest scale signed by
Taiwan. The main contents of ECFA include tax-cutting and tax
exemption policies, investment protection and intellectual property
protection. With the signing of ECFA, in a phased progression, the
tariffs of most industrial products sold by Taiwan to Mainland China
will drop to the zero level, procedures of investment will be greatly
simplified, and the scope of investment in the logistics industry will
extend into railway, port and other infrastructures. The cooperation
and integration between cross-strait logistics enterprises also will be
further deepened, and will assuredly play an important role in
promoting the development of the cross-strait logistics industry.

As the first pilot zone for cross-strait communication and cooperation, the Taiwan Strait West Coast Economic Zone is being constructed
to connect cross-strait logistics centers and build a comprehensive logistics network. This will surely improve the infrastructure and logistics
channels of the region and greatly facilitate cross-strait economic
activities.

7.6 Development of Low-Carbon Logistics

China successively promised to save energy and reduce emissions at the United Nations Summit on Climate Change and the Copenhagen Conference on Climate Change — carbon dioxide emissions per GDP in 2020 shall be decreased by 40–45% compared with that in 2005, which, as a binding index, is listed in the mid- and long-term national economic and social development plan. Hence, China will earnestly develop low-carbon technology, popularize high-efficiency, energy-saving technology and construct an industrial structure and consumption model featuring low-carbon emission.

As an industry with huge energy consumption and even higher emissions of carbon, the logistics industry has an energy consumption level per unit of added value which is higher than that of the national average. Promoting low-carbon logistics includes adopting high-efficiency, energy-saving vehicles, rationalizing transportation routes, reducing the use of packaging in logistics processes and so on. These measures are in accord with the developmental demand of a low-carbon economy and are helpful for controlling the costs of logistics enterprises. Therefore, low-carbon logistics has a wide-open future in China.

Index